PRAISE FOR *THE SECRET LIVES OF INTROVERTS*

"Jenn Granneman is among the most sensitive and thoughtful introvert authors today . . . *The Secret Lives of Introverts* brings to life the experiences every introvert shares and helps us embrace our quiet nature in a very loud world."

—Susan Cain, author of *Quiet: The Power of Introverts in a World that Can't Stop Talking* and creator of *Quiet Revolution*

"Introverts love secrets, and here, Jenn Granneman opens us to a rich world of them—secrets about what introverts think, desire, and feel; how our brains operate; why we get hangovers without drinking; how to navigate love and work; and what liberates us. An intimate line to the wisdom of introverts—without the awkward introduction and small talk."

—Laurie Helgoe, PhD, author of *Introvert Power: Why Your Inner Life is Your Hidden Strength*

"Reading Jenn Granneman's *The Secret Lives of Introverts* is like sitting on a stoop with a friend who understands the stigmas you face as an introvert. She offers you support and gentle guidance to navigate this noisy world. . . . Granneman combines compelling anecdotes and the latest research for a fact-filled and enjoyable read, succeeding at her mission to let introverts everywhere know that it?s okay to be who they are."

—Nancy Ancowitz, presentation and career coach and author of *Self-Promotion for Introverts®*

"Provides introverts and those close to them with validating insight regarding their nature. It clears many of the common misconceptions surrounding introversion. It's a wonderful in-depth guide that lets introverts know we are not alone in our way of being, while informing those less introverted of our strengths, gifts, and ability to be happy as we are."

—Brenda Knowles, creator of Space2Live and author of *The Quiet Rise of Introverts: 8 Practices for Living and Loving in a Noisy World*

"This one goes out to all of us who have a still surface but depths that teem with energy and life. Allow [Jenn Granneman] to show you the magic of your inner worlds and how to quietly bless others with what stirs down deep."

—Adam S. McHugh, author of *Introverts in the Church* and *The Listening Life*

"*The Secret Lives of Introverts* is the new introvert's bible containing everything you need to know to understand, embrace, and celebrate your introversion. Granneman strikes a blissful balance between intriguing research on the science of introversion and heartfelt personal stories and insights that will have you shouting 'amen' in agreement (in your head, of course). True to her introverted nature, Granneman takes a thoughtful and thorough approach to explaining the many intricacies of being an introvert in an extrovert-biased world."

—Michaela Chung, author of *The Irresistible Introvert:*
Harness The Power of Quiet Charisma in a Loud World

"Jenn Granneman conveys everything that is beautiful and unique about what it means to be an introvert. She guides us through some difficult moments in life that are all too familiar to anyone who has struggled coming to terms with their quiet personality."

—Debbie Tung, author of *Quiet Girl in a Noisy World*
and creator of *Where's My Bubble*

"*The Secret Lives of Introverts* is a book for everyone, introverts and extroverts alike. From the first embrace of chapter one, introverts who have endured the pain of feeling out of place, inadequate, or outright weird will feel remarkably understood. . . . Jenn's warmth and exceptional ability to connect with her readers makes *The Secret Lives of Introverts* an enjoyable, validating, and encouraging must read. I love this book, and you will too!"

—Aaron Caycedo-Kimura, author of *Text, Don't Call:*
An Illustrated Guide to the Introverted Life

"One of the best books I've ever read on introvert empowerment. Granneman's fearless honesty about what it means to be an introvert in today's loud, fast, and busy world filled with overcrowded schedules and spaces is desperately needed by all of us who have ever felt 'too sensitive.' She's given me my new personal mantra: 'In your alone time, you're free.'"

—Lauren Sapala, author of *The INFJ Writer*

"Reading this book was like finding a decoder ring for introverts. Jenn Granneman's candid, eloquent description of the introvert experience had me nodding along and underlining parts. It's wonderful to know that we are not alone, even in our need for solitude and quiet."

—Nanea Hoffman, founder of *Sweatpants & Coffee*

"*The Secret Lives of Introverts* is for every introvert who has felt different. Filled with practical advice just for introverts on everything from romance to careers . . . its pages are filled with "mhm" moments and "aha" insights."

—Thea Orozco, visibility advisor at *Introvertology*

The Secret Lives of
INTROVERTS

Inside Our
Hidden World

Jenn Granneman

Skyhorse Publishing

Skyhorse Publishing books may be purchased in bulk at special discounts for sales promotion, corporate gifts, fund-raising, or educational purposes. Special editions can also be created to specifications. For details, contact the Special Sales Department, Skyhorse Publishing, 307 West 36th Street, 11th Floor, New York, NY 10018 or info@skyhorsepublishing.com.

Skyhorse® and Skyhorse Publishing® are registered trademarks of Skyhorse Publishing, Inc.®, a Delaware corporation.

Visit our website at www.skyhorsepublishing.com.

10 9 8 7

Library of Congress Cataloging-in-Publication Data is available on file.

Cover design by Jane Sheppard
Cover photo credit: iStockphoto
Illustrations by Adrianne Lee

Print ISBN: 978-1-5107-2102-9
Ebook ISBN: 978-1-5107-2103-6

Printed in the United States of America

DEDICATION

This book is dedicated to my grandpa, John Granneman, and my uncle, Dave Granneman, who both passed away while I was writing it. Grandpa John loved studying the Wild West, drinking black coffee, reading the newspaper end to end, and rolling his own cigarettes at the kitchen table. He was a quiet man who didn't say much, and he once confided in me that he had always been an introvert. Uncle Dave loved a good conspiracy theory and tales of UFOs, and if you got him going, he could really talk. He was half extrovert, half legend.

John Granneman
April 23, 1925, to January 23, 2017

David Granneman
April 12, 1949, to February 25, 2017

CONTENTS

INTRODUCTION

Dear introvert,

One of my earliest memories as a little girl is my dad putting a microphone to my lips and asking me to tell a story. *Okay,* I thought, *this should be easy.* I had been telling stories to myself already, in my mind, each night before I fell asleep, even though I was too young to read or write.

I closed my eyes and imagined a horse who played with her friends in a sunny meadow. Like many introverted children, my inner world was vivid and alive. The made-up story seemed almost as real as the actual world around me of toys and parents and pets. The horse and her friends were having a race to see who was the fastest. They dashed through fields of flowers and jumped over a glistening creek, when, all of the sudden, one of them started to flap her tiny, hidden wings and fly . . .

Suddenly, my dad interrupted my thoughts. "You have to say your story out loud," he said, nodding to the microphone. "So I can record it."

I looked at the microphone, then back at my dad, but I didn't know how to respond. The things inside me had to be spoken? How could mere words describe the striking images I saw in my mind—and how they made me feel?

Sensing my hesitancy, my dad prompted again. "Just say what you're thinking," he said, as if that were the easiest thing in the world.

But I couldn't. I continued to stare at my dad in silence. The secret world inside me would not come out. My dad grew impatient, probably thinking his only daughter was being stubborn, uncreative. The truth was I had no idea how to translate my inner experience into words. Somehow, I thought that with my father's supreme intelligence, he would just know what I meant to say. But he couldn't read my thoughts. And the microphone attached to the primitive eighties tape recorder couldn't hear them. Eventually, he gave up and put everything away.

This would not be the last time in my life that my silence confused and frustrated someone. I would carry that feeling of disconnect between my inner world and the outer one with me for much of my life.

If you're an introvert like me, you may have secrets inside you, too. You have thoughts that you don't have the words to express and big ideas that no one else sees. Maybe your secret is you feel lonely even when you're surrounded by other people. Perhaps you're doing certain things and acting a certain way only because you think you're *supposed* to. Maybe your heart longs for just one person to see the real you—and to know what's really going on inside your head.

This is a book about secrets. It's about seeing what's really going on with introverts. It's about finally feeling understood.

Thank you for joining me in this journey. If you have a secret like the one I just described, I hope you will feel less alone about it after reading this book.

Quietly yours,

Jenn

Chapter 1

THIS IS FOR ALL THE QUIET ONES

When I was in sixth grade, I was lucky enough to be scooped up by a great group of girls who would become my lifelong friends. We slept over at each other's houses and whispered secrets in the dark. We spied on the boy who lived in the neighborhood and his friends, and giggled over who we had crushes on. We filled notebook after notebook with our dreams for the future. We even promised to reunite every Fourth of July as adults on a hill by our high school, so we would always have a place in each other's lives.

Anyone looking at us would have thought I was just one of the girls. We did almost everything together. People even said we looked like sisters. But deep down, I felt different. I wasn't one of them. I was *other*.

While they read *Seventeen* magazine and chatted about celebrities, I sat silently on the edges, wondering if there was life on other planets. When they were relieved that another school year was over and that summer vacation had begun, I was catapulted into a deep existential crisis about growing older. When they wanted to hang out all night, and then the next day, and then the *next*, I was desperately searching for an excuse to be alone. ("Mom, tell them I'm sick! Or that I have to go to church!") In so many little ways, I was the weird one.

My friend group was the center of my teenage world. I *loved* them. So I did what anyone does when they feel like they are an alien dropped into this world from another planet: at times, I pretended. I kept my secret thoughts to myself. I didn't let on when I wished I could be alone in my bedroom instead of at the mall, surrounded by people. I tried to be the person I thought I *should* be—fun-loving and always ready to hang out.

All that pretending got exhausting. But I did it because I thought that's what everyone else was doing—pretending. I figured they were just a lot better at hiding their true feelings than I was.

There Must Be Something Wrong with Me

As an adult, I still couldn't shake the feeling of being "different." I worked as a journalist for a few years, then went back to school to become a teacher, thinking this would be more meaningful work. My graduate program was full of outgoing would-be teachers who always had something to say. They sat in little groups on breaks, bursting with energetic chatter, even after we'd just spent hours doing collaborative learning or having a group discussion. I, on the other hand, bolted for the door on breaks as quickly as possible—my head was spinning from all the noise and activity, and my energy level was at zero. Also, talking in front of our class or answering a question on the spot was no problem for them. I, however, avoided the spotlight as much as possible. Whenever I had to present a lesson plan, I felt compelled to practice exactly what I was going to say, until I got it "perfect." Even then, I usually couldn't keep my hands from shaking.

I had also gotten married. My husband (now ex-husband) was a confident, life-of-the-party guy who could talk to anyone. His large family was the same way. They loved spending time together in a loud gaggle of kids, siblings, and friends of the family. Often, they'd drop by our small apartment, letting me know they were coming only when they were already on their way. They'd pass hours crammed into the living room, telling stories, cracking jokes, and volleying sarcastic remarks back and forth with the professional finesse of Venus and Serena Williams. I, once again, sat quietly on the edges, never knowing how to wedge myself into these fast-moving conversations or what to say. As the night wore on, I often found myself slipping into an exhausted brain fog, which made it even harder to participate. Most nights, what I really wanted was to read a book alone, play a video game, or just be with my husband.

When comparing myself to my extroverted in-laws and classmates, I never seemed to measure up. My disparaging thoughts returned. Why couldn't I just loosen up and go with the flow? Why did I never have much to say when I was in a big group but had plenty to talk about during a one-on-one? Why was my idea of a good time so different from what other people wanted to do?

I was broken. I had to be.

Things didn't look like they would ever get better. At one point, I had a complete breakdown. I found myself awake in the middle of the night, frantically crying, typing everything that was wrong with me and my life into a Word document. I just couldn't take it anymore. I was too different—too messed up. The world was too much, too loud, too harsh. I think finally expressing all the secret feelings that had built up inside me—in a raw, unfiltered way—saved me. When I reread what I had written, I realized I couldn't keep living this way.

Somehow, I made it through that terrible night. Soon after, I discovered something about myself that changed my life.

One Magic Word: *Introvert*

One afternoon, in the psychology/self-help section of a used bookstore, I came across a book called *The Introvert Advantage* by Marti Olsen Laney. I bought it and read it cover to cover. When I finished, I cried. I had never felt so understood in my life.

That beautiful book told me there was a word for what I was: *introvert*. It was a magic word, because it explained many of the things I had struggled with my entire life—things that had made me feel bad about myself. Best of all, the word meant I wasn't alone. There were other people out there like me. Other introverts.

Say what you will about labeling. That little label changed my life.

I went on to read everything about introversion I could get my hands on. I read *Quiet* by Susan Cain, *Introvert Power* by Laurie Helgoe, *The Introvert's Way* by Sophia Dembling, and others. I became interested in personality type and high sensitivity, too. Turns out I'm not just an introvert but also a highly sensitive person (but I'll leave that topic for another time). After reading dozens of books about introversion, I turned to the Internet. I joined Facebook groups for introverts and poured over blogs. My friends got sick of me constantly talking about introversion: "Did you know it's an *introvert thing* to need time to think before responding?" I'd say, or, "I can't go out tonight, it's *introvert time.*"

I couldn't shut up about being an introvert. It was like I had been reading the wrong script my entire life, trying to play the role of the person I thought I *should* be—not the person I truly was.

Don't get me wrong. Learning about my introversion didn't fix all my problems. It would take several years of hard, inner work—along with consciously deciding to make real changes in my life—before things got better. But for me, embracing my introversion—and stopping myself from trying to pretend to be an extrovert—was the first step. As I learned more about introversion, I became more confident in who I was. I started accepting my need for alone time. I saw my quiet, reflective nature as a strength, not a liability. I also started working on my social skills, seeing them as simply that—skills I could improve and use to my advantage. But most important, for the first time in my life, I started to actually like myself.

I was no longer an *other*. I was something else: an introvert.

Now I'm on a Mission

Today, I'm the voice behind *Introvert, Dear,* the popular online community for introverts. I never set out to be an advocate for introverts, but, when something changes your life, you want to tell other people about it. I started *Introvert, Dear* as my personal blog in 2013. At the time, I was working as a teacher, living with roommates, and truly dating for the first time in my adult life. I decided I would chronicle my life as an introvert living in a society that seems geared toward extroverts. I kept my blog anonymous so I could write whatever I wanted without fearing what other people would think (so very introverted of me). For my bio, I used a picture of just my shoulder that showed off a tattoo of five birds I had just gotten. My face was mostly hidden.

Staring at my computer screen, alone in my bedroom one night, I named my little blog *Introvert, Dear*. I imagined a wise, older introverted woman counseling a younger introverted woman. The young woman was lying on a chaise lounge, and the older woman was sitting in a chair nearby, the kind of setup you see in movies when someone goes to a therapist. The older one began her advice to the younger one by saying, "Now, introvert, *dear . . .*"

The first blog post I wrote got more comments about my tattoo than anything actually related to what I'd written. But I kept writing, mostly just for myself. And people kept reading. I didn't know it then, but *Introvert, Dear* was another step in my journey toward healing. Once again, expressing myself honestly relieved some of the pain I was feeling. And connecting with other introverts made me feel less self-conscious about my "weird" ways.

Today, *Introvert, Dear* is less of a blog and more of an online publishing platform. It features not just my voice, but hundreds of introvert voices, and it brings together introverts from all over the world. My writing about introverts has been featured in publications like the *Huffington Post*, *Thought Catalog*, Susan Cain's *Quiet Revolution*, the *Mighty*, and others. Now I'm on a mission: to let introverts everywhere know it's okay to be who they are. I don't ever want another introvert to feel the way I did when I was younger.

Are You an Introvert?

What about you? Have you always felt different? Were you the quiet one in school? Did people ask you, "Why don't you talk more?" Do they still ask you that today?

If so, you might be an introvert like me. Introverts make up 30 to 50 percent of the population, and we help shape the world we live in. We might be your parent, friend, spouse, significant other, child, or coworker. We lead, create, educate, innovate, do business, solve problems, charm, heal, and love. Introversion is a temperament, which is different from your personality; temperament refers to your inborn traits that organize how you approach the world, while personality can be defined as the pattern of behavior, thoughts, and emotions that make you an individual. It can take years to build a personality, but your temperament is something you're born with.

But the most important thing to know about being an introvert is that there's nothing wrong with you. You're not broken because you're quiet. It's okay to stay home on a Friday night instead of going to a party. Being an introvert is a perfectly normal "thing" to be.

Are you an introvert? Here are twenty-two signs that you might veer toward introversion on the spectrum. How many do you relate to? These signs may not apply to every introvert, but I believe they are generally true:

1. **You enjoy spending time alone.** You have no problem staying home on a Saturday night. In fact, you look forward to it. To you, Netflix and chill *really means* watching Netflix and relaxing. Or maybe your thing is reading, playing video games, drawing, cooking, writing, knitting tiny hats for cats, or just lounging around the house. Whatever your preferred solo activity is, you do it as much as your schedule allows. You feel good when you're alone. In your alone time, you're free.

2. **You do your best thinking when you're alone.** Your alone time isn't just about indulging in your favorite hobbies. It's about giving your mind time to decompress. When you're with other people, it may feel like your brain is too overloaded to really work the way it should. In solitude, you're free to tune into your own inner monologue, rather than paying attention to what's going on around you. You might be more creative and/or have deeper insights when you're alone.

3. **Your inner monologue never stops.** You have a distinct inner voice that's always running in the back of your mind. If people could hear the thoughts that ran through your head, they may, in turn, be surprised, amazed, and perhaps horrified. Whatever their reaction might be, your inner narrator is something that's hard to shut off. Sometimes you can't sleep at night because your mind is still going. Thoughts from your past haunt you. "I can't believe I said that stupid thing . . . five years ago!"

4. **You often feel lonelier in a crowd than when you're alone.** There's something about being with a group that makes you feel disconnected from yourself. Maybe it's because it's hard to hear your inner voice when there's so much noise around you. Or maybe you feel like an *other*, like I did. Whatever the reason, as an introvert, you crave intimate moments and deep connections—and those usually aren't found in a crowd.

5. **You feel like you're faking it when you have to network.** Walking up to strangers and introducing yourself? You'd rather stick tiny needles under your fingernails. But you know there's value in it, so you might do it anyway—except you feel like a phony the entire time. If you're anything like me, you had to teach yourself how to do it. You might have read self-help books about how to be a better conversationalist or exude more charisma. In the moment, you have to activate your "public persona." You might say things to yourself like, "Smile, make eye contact, and use your loud-confident voice!" Then, when you're finished, you feel beat, and you need downtime to recover. You wonder, *Does everyone else have to try this hard when meeting new people?*

6. **You're not the student shooting your hand up every time the teacher asks a question.** You don't need all that attention. You're content just *knowing* that you know the answer—you don't have to prove it to anyone else. At work, this may translate to not saying much during meetings. You'd rather pull your boss aside afterward and have a one-on-one conversation, or email your ideas, rather than explain them to a room full of people. The exception to this is when you feel truly passionate about something. On rare occasions, even shy introverts have been known to transform themselves into a force to be reckoned with when it really counts. It's all about how much something matters to you; you'll risk overstimulation when you think speaking up will truly make a difference.

7. **You're better at writing your thoughts than speaking them.** You prefer texting to calling and emailing to face-to-face meetings. Writing gives you time to reflect on what to say and how to say it. It allows you to edit your thoughts and craft your message just so. Plus, there's less pressure when you're typing your words into your phone alone than when you're saying them to someone in real time. But it isn't just about texting and emailing. Many introverts enjoy journaling for self-expression and self-discovery. Others make a career out of writing, such as John Green, author of the bestselling young adult novel, *The Fault in Our Stars.* In his YouTube video, "Thoughts from Places: The Tour," Green says, "Writing is something you do alone. It's a profession for introverts who want to tell you a story but don't want to make eye contact while doing it."

8. **Likewise, talking on the phone does not sound like a fun way to pass the time.** One of my extroverted friends is always calling me when she's alone in her car. She figures that although her eyes, hands, and feet are currently occupied, her mouth is not. Plus, there are no people around— how boring! So she reaches for her phone. (Remember to practice safe driving, kids.) However, this is not the case for me. When I have a few spare minutes of silence and solitude, I have no desire to fill that time with idle chitchat.

9. **You'd rather not engage with people who are angry.** Psychologist Marta Ponari and collaborators found that people high in introversion don't show what's called the

"gaze-cueing effect." Normally, if you were to view the image of a person's face on a computer screen looking in a certain direction, you would follow that person's gaze; therefore, you'd respond more quickly to a visual target on that side of the screen than when the person's gaze and the target point in opposite directions. Introverts and extroverts both do this, with one exception: if the person seems mad, introverts don't show the gaze-cueing effect. This suggests that people who are very introverted don't want to look at someone who seems angry. Ponari and her team think that this is because they are more sensitive to potentially negative evaluations. Meaning, if you think a person is mad because of something related to you, even their gaze becomes a threat.

10. **You avoid small talk whenever possible.** When a coworker is walking down the hall toward you, have you ever turned into another room in order to avoid having a "Hey, what's up?" conversation with them? Or have you ever waited a few minutes in your apartment when you heard your neighbors in the hallway so you didn't have to chat? If so, you might be an introvert, because introverts tend to avoid small talk. We'd rather talk about something meaningful than fill the air with chatter just to hear ourselves make noise. We find small talk inauthentic, and, frankly, many of us feel awkward doing it.

11. **You've been told you're "too intense."** This stems from your dislike of small talk. If it were up to you, mindless chitchat would be banished. You'd much rather sit down

with someone and discuss the meaning of life—or, at the very least, exchange some real, honest thoughts. Have you ever had a deep conversation and walked away feeling energized, not drained? That's what I'm talking about. Meaningful interactions are the introvert's antidote to social burnout.

12. **You don't go to parties to meet new people.** Birthday parties, wedding receptions, staff holiday parties, or whatever—you party every once in a while. But when you go to an event, you probably don't go with the goal of making new friends; you'd rather hang out with the people you already know. That's because, like a pair of well-worn sneakers, your current friends feel good on you. They know your quirks, and you feel comfortable around them. Plus, making new friends would mean making small talk.

13. **You shut down after too much socializing.** A study from Finnish researchers Sointu Leikas and Ville-Juhani Ilmarinen shows that socializing eventually becomes tiring to both introverts *and* extroverts. That's likely because socializing expends energy. Not only do you have to talk, but you also have to listen and process what's being said. Plus, you're taking in all kinds of sensory information, such as someone's tone of voice and body language—along with filtering out any background noises or visual distractions. It's no wonder people get drained. But there are some very real differences between introverts and extroverts; on average, introverts really do prefer solitude and quiet more than their extroverted counterparts. In fact, if you're an introvert,

you might experience something that's been dubbed the "introvert hangover." Like a hangover induced by one too many giant fishbowl margaritas, you feel sluggish and icky after too much socializing. Your brain seems to stop working, and, in your exhaustion, you cease to be able to hold a conversation or say words that make sense. You just want to lie down in a quiet, dark room and not move or talk for a while. That's because introverts can become overstimulated by socializing and shut down (more about the introvert hangover later).

14. **You notice details that others miss.** It's true that introverts (especially highly sensitive introverts) can get overwhelmed by too much stimuli. But there's an upside to our sensitivity—we notice details that others might miss. For example, you might notice a subtle change in your friend's demeanor signaling that she's upset (but oddly, no one else in the room sees it). Or, you might be highly tuned in to color, space, and texture, making you an incredible visual artist.

15. **You can concentrate for long periods of time on things that matter to you.** I can write for hours. I get in the zone, and I just keep going. I don't need anyone or anything else to entertain me—as I write, I enter a state of flow. I block out distractions and hone in on what I need to accomplish. If you're an introvert, you likely have activities or pet projects that you could work on for practically forever. That's because introverts are great at focusing alone for long

periods of time. If it weren't for introverts and our amazing ability to focus, we wouldn't have the theory of relativity, Google, or Harry Potter (yes, Einstein, Larry Page, and J. K. Rowling are all likely introverts). Dear society, where would you be without us? You're welcome. Love, introverts.

16. **You live in your head.** In fact, you may daydream so much that people have told you to "get out of your head" or "come down to earth." That's because your inner world is rich and vivid. Not all introverts have strong imaginations (that trait is correlated with "openness to experience" on the Big Five personality scale, not "extroversion-introversion"), but many of us do.

17. **You like to people watch.** Actually, you just like to observe in general, whether it's people, nature, etc. Introverts are natural observers. They can often be found hanging out along the edges of a party or event, just watching, rather than in the thick of things.

18. **You've been told you're a good listener.** You don't mind giving the stage to someone else for a bit and listening. You're not clamoring to get every thought out there, because you don't need to "talk to think" or vocalize everything that crosses your mind the way some extroverts do. Listening—truly listening—means you get to learn something new or better understand what makes someone tick.

19. **You have a small circle of friends.** You're close with just one, two, or three people, and you consider everyone else

to be an acquaintance. That's because introverts only have so much "people" energy to spend, so we choose our relationships carefully. It's about budgeting.

20. **You don't get "high" off your environment.** There's a reason why crowds, parties, and networking events aren't your thing: introverts and extroverts differ in how their brains process experiences through reward centers. Neurobiologists Yu Fu and Richard Depue demonstrated this phenomenon by giving Ritalin to introverted and extroverted college students (Ritalin is a drug used to treat ADHD that stimulates the production of the feel-good neurotransmitter dopamine in the brain). They found that extroverts were more likely to connect their feelings of bliss with the environment they were in. However, introverts did not associate the feeling of reward with their surroundings. This suggests that introverts have a basic difference in how strongly they process rewards from their environment (more about introverts and rewards later). According to the researchers, the brains of introverts may weigh internal cues more strongly than external ones. In other words, introverts don't feel "high" from their surroundings; instead, we're paying more attention to what's going on inwardly.

21. **You're an old soul.** Introverts tend to observe, process information deeply, and reflect before they speak. Analytical by nature, we're often interested in discovering the deeper meaning or underlying pattern behind events. Because of this, introverts can seem wise, even from a young age.

22. **You alternate between being with people and being alone.** Introverts relish being alone. In our solitude, we have the freedom to tune into our inner voice and tune out the noise of the world; as we do this, we gain energy and clarity. But introverts don't always want to be alone. As human beings, we're wired to connect with others, and as introverts, we long to connect meaningfully. So introverts live in two worlds: we visit the world of people, but solitude and the inner world will always be our home.

Still Not Sure?

Still not sure if you're an introvert? Here's a quick test. Answer these two questions honestly:

1. If you had to choose between two options for a dream vacation, which one would you pick?
    A) A relaxing vacation by yourself or with just one other person, a good book, and a secluded cabin.
    B) A group vacation with your friends or family, doing exciting things, like gambling in Las Vegas or partying on a cruise ship.

Don't think about what you *should* do or what's expected of you. Which one would you pick if you didn't care what anyone else thought about you? As you probably guessed, if you chose the secluded cabin, you're more of an introvert. If you picked the second option, you're probably more extroverted.

2. Imagine your dream day. What activities would you do?
   Who would you want to hang out with?

If your perfect day consists of doing something low-key with just one or two people—or alone—you're probably an introvert. If you imagine yourself surrounded by lots of people doing something active, you're probably more of an extrovert.

Keep in mind that introversion and extroversion are not all-or-nothing traits. Imagine a spectrum with introversion on one end and extroversion on the other. Everyone lands somewhere on that spectrum, with some falling closer to the introverted end and others nearer the extroverted end. Nobody is a pure introvert or extrovert. "Such a person would be in the lunatic asylum," wrote Carl Jung, the famous Swiss psychologist who first coined the term *introvert*. In other words, we all act "extroverted" in some situations and "introverted" in others. For example, when I'm with my close friends, I talk, laugh, argue, and sometimes even dance. It's because I feel comfortable with them—but I'm still an introvert who needs plenty of alone time.

When writing this book, I talked with hundreds of introverts. True to introvert fashion, many of those "conversations" happened in writing, via email and social media. In a few instances, I was lucky enough to be able to sit down with someone and interview that person face-to-face. Throughout this book, I share comments from the introverts I interviewed, as well as research studies, my own experiences, and stories that have been published on IntrovertDear.com. As an introvert, you may find yourself identifying with some parts of this book but not with others. Let me be clear: that's perfectly okay.

Just because you don't relate to everything doesn't mean you're not an introvert. There's no wrong way to do introversion.

Tips for Extroverts

Do I spy an extrovert? Don't think I didn't see you, hanging out in my introvert book (most extroverts *loooove* being wherever there are people). But don't worry, you're welcome here, too. In fact, I've included tips in most chapters just for you to help you understand introverts better. Look for tips in a box like this one. Whether you're an extrovert in a relationship with an introvert, the coworker of an introvert, the family member of an introvert, or the friend of an introvert, there's something in this book for you, too.

Why I Wrote This Book

For too long, introverts have been misunderstood. We may have been the ones who were bullied on the playground as kids for being too "different." We may have great ideas but lack the self-confidence to say them out loud. We've been told we're too quiet, too sensitive, or too shy. When we say we're staying in tonight, pained looks from our friends tell us there's something wrong with us. Conversations whispered by the adults of our childhood told us we are seriously broken.

Keia, for example, is an introvert who feels like an outsider at work. "People always seem to think I'm upset or that I don't want to be bothered, and, in some instances, it's true," she tells me.

"I don't mind chatting every once in a while, but I feel as though I do my best work when I'm silent and focused." Her coworkers don't understand her need for quiet. In fact, things have gotten pretty tense with them at times. They say things to her like, "You're so quiet," or, "You need to open up more." This really frustrates Keia, because like many introverts, she's at work to, well, *work*. Not make friends.

She wonders why she needs to talk more. She does her job well. She doesn't dislike her coworkers. "I just enjoy being by myself," she says. "I enjoy thinking and being in my own little world. It relaxes me, and I feel free. Sometimes people make me feel like I'm some sort of criminal for being an introvert. I wish that work environments were more supportive of people like us. We don't mean any harm."

Amanda is another introvert who feels out of place. When she started college, she hadn't yet identified as an introvert. However, it quickly became obvious that she was different from the other students. After class, instead of going back to the dorms and cramming herself into someone's tiny room with a dozen other co-eds to hang out, she'd sneak off by herself. She discovered a little park near campus and she'd spend hours there, studying or reading.

"I didn't know why I did this or what it did for me," she tells me. "I just needed to be by myself. I wasn't shy or antisocial. I certainly didn't know my time in the park was replenishing my energy or why I craved time alone when my friends didn't."

After spending time in the park, she could head back to the dorms and "survive the never-ending social interaction" that awaited her. But in the back of her mind, she knew other students weren't doing this. Why was she so different?

And finally, there's Justin. In college, he took a communications course. He knew, of course, that communication is so much more than just talking. But right away, he felt out of place. His class seemed to be full of extroverts who knew how to do only two things: talk loudly—and a lot.

"Everyone seemed to fit in, chatting here and there," he tells me. "When someone noticed me being the only quiet person in the room, he asked me why. I told him, 'Hey, I'm an introvert. I don't feel the need to always talk.'" The classmate looked at him like he was an alien from another planet and asked him in a snarky tone why he bothered to enroll in a course about communication. Justin just smiled, and never said another word to him.

Why did I write this book? I wrote it for Keia, Amanda, and Justin. I wrote it for my introverted twelve-year-old self who got drained after hanging out with her friends and didn't know why. I wrote it for all the members of the *Introvert, Dear* community. Most important, I wrote this book for you.

This is for all the quiet ones.

It's time to change how the world sees introverts. It's time to change how we introverts see ourselves. And I'll tell you a secret: it all starts when you begin working *with* your introversion, rather than *fighting against it*. I'll show you how. Read on.

Chapter 2

THE SCIENCE OF INTROVERSION

Has something like this ever happened to you? You're at a party or some get-together. The room is full of people, music is playing, and it's *loud.* You do your best to be friendly, making small talk even though you'd rather be at home binge-watching your latest Netflix obsession. Everyone around you looks like they're having a good time, so you smile and laugh, too—you don't want to stick out. But after a while, all the noise and chatter become too much, so you retreat to an empty couch in a deserted corner of the room where you take a break by sitting quietly. From back here, you watch everything. It kind of becomes fun to be a silent observer. You notice little things you didn't notice before, and your mind analyzes it all. Sitting quietly, you feel your energy returning.

If you're an introvert, you probably know what happens next. It doesn't take long for someone to spot you sitting alone. Usually it's an extrovert. They plop down next to you, invading your quiet sanctuary. Then comes the dreaded question: "Are you okay?"

You pause, unsure of how to answer. You could be honest, explaining, "I'm an introvert, and I needed to take a break from socializing." But more likely, since you're caught off guard and now feeling self-conscious, you release a panicked, "Yeah! Everything's fine."

The extrovert gives you a strange look. They may raise an eyebrow in confusion. You sigh internally and head back to the crowd.

This sort of thing has happened to me many times. And when it did, I didn't understand it. At parties, happy hours, and group dinners, everyone around me seemed to be having a good time. In fact, they seemed to be getting *more* energetic as the night went on. Why was I the only one showing signs of burnout? Today, I know a secret: it has to do with the way introverts are wired.

In this chapter, we'll explore the science behind introversion. I'll answer the question, "Why do introverts get drained from socializing?" and several other questions about the nature of introverts. I hope learning about the science behind your quiet temperament helps you understand yourself better and inspires you to further love who you are.

The Sex, Drugs, and Rock 'n' Roll Molecule

The reason introverts and extroverts react to things differently—like partying—has to do with a chemical found in the brain called dopamine. Dopamine is sometimes called the "sex, drugs, and rock 'n' roll" molecule because it helps control the brain's pleasure and reward centers. That's a catchy description, but it's not entirely accurate. Dopamine itself doesn't guarantee that you'll feel pleasure. What it does guarantee is you'll be excited by the *possibility* of pleasure. In a restaurant, when a server shows you a tray of tantalizing desserts and you get excited about eating one, that's dopamine at work.

Introverts and extroverts both have dopamine in their brains. The difference is extroverts have a more active dopamine reward system than introverts, according to Scott Barry Kaufman, the scientific director of the Imagination Institute. In other words, simply put, when extroverts see potential rewards, they get more excited about them than introverts. Rewards are things like social attention, social status, money, food, and sexual opportunities (and yes, what you've always suspected is true—research from a university in West Germany shows that extroverts really do tend to have more sex than introverts, though whether or not the sex is as good or as fulfilling is the second part of the question).

If you're excited about the possibility of something, you'll have more energy and motivation to pursue it. In other words, dopamine helps reduce your cost of effort. This is why extroverts are often found chatting enthusiastically with strangers, calling attention to themselves in groups, and making bold moves—without getting as worn out as introverts would. Introverts, on the other hand, just aren't as energized by potential rewards in their environment—especially social rewards. The possibilities of making a new friend or becoming popular just aren't as exciting to us. This also explains why introverts feel drained after socializing. Unlike extroverts, we don't get a "cost of effort" reduction.

A study conducted in 2005 by Michael Cohen and his colleagues found a link between extroversion and dopamine. For the study, they asked participants to perform a gambling task while they were in a brain scanner. It will probably come as no surprise to you that the imaging data showed that brain activity differed between extroverts and introverts. When a gamble paid off, the extroverts showed a stronger response in two brain regions: the nucleus accumbens and the amygdala. The nucleus accumbens plays a key role in the brain's reward circuitry and is part of the dopamine system. The amygdala processes emotional stimuli. Cohen's results provide evidence for the theory that introverts process rewards differently than extroverts.

Too Loud, Too Many People

Another way to understand introversion is to think about it in terms of stimulation. Simply put, stimulation is anything registered by your senses—things you see, hear, taste, touch, and smell. Because introverts are not as energized by potential rewards, they may find levels of stimulation that are rewarding for extroverts to be simply tiring or annoying, according to Colin DeYoung, a psychology professor at the University of Minnesota. Think: a loud rock concert with tons of people, a crowded bar on a Saturday night, or a busy casino with lots of flashing lights. If you're an introvert like me, you can probably put up with these environments for a short period of time. You may even have fun for a while. But eventually, you become overstimulated and feel drained. That's when you want to run for home where it's calm and quiet.

Stimulation can also come in the form of socializing. Think about everything that happens during a conversation. You make eye contact with the person who is talking, and you listen to what they say. Their words are incoming stimulation

AN INTROVERT AND AN EXTROVERT... ...GO TO A PARTY...

ELLIE EXTROVERT   IZZY INTROVERT

THIS IS AWESOME!
BRING IT!

RECOGNITION!

NEW FRIENDS

PRAISE!

FLIRTY STRANGER!

ADMIRATION!

UMMM... CAN I GET A
SMALLER DOSE, PLEASE?

CUTE GUY!

ATTENTION!

NEW FRIENDS

LOUD MUSIC!

that you have to process, reflect on, and respond to. You're probably also using brain power to monitor your tone of voice and body language, as well as paying attention to theirs, trying to "read" what it means. If you're in a group, there are even more people to pay attention to. No wonder cocktail parties and happy hours get tiring for introverts.

For Extroverts: It's All about Dosage

If your introverted friend or partner wants to leave a party—or not go in the first place—they're not doing this just to be difficult. Because introverts respond differently to rewards, we don't gain as much energy from socializing as you do. Simply put, the big social event isn't as fun for us. So, cut your introvert some slack and see if the two of you can compromise. Can you go to the party but let the introvert decide when it's time to leave? Or can the introvert sit this one out—leaving you to party as long as you want? Better yet, can the two of you drive separately, so you can stay as late as you want but the introvert can leave when they feel burned out? Introverts can enjoy socializing, but it's all about dosage. Too much noise and too many people, and introverts get overstimulated.

How Introverts Feel Rewarded

Introverts may not get high on shaking hands with strangers, but that doesn't mean we don't feel rewarded in other ways. I asked introverts to tell me what types of activities energize and reward them. Not surprisingly, they all said they like doing something alone or with just a few other people whose company they really enjoy.

"A reward I enjoy is dinner alone. I even dress up nice. Or a bike ride around the city. Alleyways are my favorite because there are so many interesting things in alleyways, and they are quieter."

—Joe

"I like socializing with one or two people I like in a low-pressure environment."

—Marissa

"I always feel rewarded when I finish a good book. Being given a chance to peer into somebody else's mind is a wondrous thing."

—Austin

"I love to go on a run where I can listen to my favorite tunes and observe my surroundings."

—Shanna

"I love just wandering my city with my headphones on and a camera."

—Piper

"Surprisingly, I like doing the dishes. It may seem monotonous, but it's very therapeutic to have time to myself where I don't have to think about what I'm doing. I can just daydream."

—Hannah

"Hiking! Nothing better than a good twelve-mile hike through the White Mountains by myself."

—Chris

"I like sitting in my bedroom listening to a good album, enjoying food in an empty restaurant, and being able to shop in peace in an empty mall."

—Tina

The Introvert's Origin Story

If you're an introvert, your dopamine reward system is not as active as your extroverted friend's or partner's. Why? Were you born this way? Or did something happen to you at some point in your life that made you like this? It's the old nature vs. nurture question. Is it your DNA or your life experiences that make you who you are?

I see introverts discussing this topic often. In comments on an *Introvert, Dear* article or in the *Introvert, Dear* Facebook group, introverts hypothesize about the "origin" of their introversion. They write things like, "I was an extrovert until I was bullied in elementary school. I lost my confidence and turned into an introvert." Or, "I was raised by introverted parents who always wanted things to be quiet. I got used to not talking much." Or even, "After my girlfriend broke up with me,

I turned into an introvert who didn't want to leave the house." Is it true? Did circumstances turn these people into introverts?

To answer that question, let's take a look at the introvert's origin story. Every superhero has an origin story. Superman was rocketed to Earth as an infant by his scientist father moments before his home planet's destruction. When a young Bruce Wayne's parents were killed, he swore an oath to rid Gotham City of evil and became Batman. What's the introvert's origin story?

To understand our origin story, first you need to understand the difference between temperament and personality. Dr. Nancy Snidman, a research professor in the Child Development Unit of the University of Massachusetts, told me in an interview that your temperament is made up of genetic and biological factors that influence how you view and respond to your environment. Remember, introversion and extroversion are temperaments. Personality, on the other hand, is a mix of both your temperament and environment. When I use the word *personality* in this book, I'm not talking about your Myers-Briggs personality type, your Enneagram, or anything like that. Instead, I mean the combination of qualities that form your unique character. It's your introversion with your life experiences piled on top.

You were probably born an introvert. From day one, you had the seed of introversion encoded in your DNA. When you were born, your dopamine reward system was less active than your extroverted peers'. As you grew, you reacted to your surroundings as an introvert. You may have been more cautious than other children, clinging to your parent's leg instead of running excitedly toward the play group.

Snidman and her colleagues see this when they study babies. About 40 percent of babies are what she calls "behaviorally uninhibited," meaning they don't react strongly when presented with unknown lights, sounds, objects, or people. They remain calm and are not disturbed by novelty. Another 15 to 20 percent of babies do the opposite. When presented with novel stimuli, they thrash their arms and legs, cry, or show other signs of behavioral arousal.

The way individuals react—whether they react strongly or not to new things—doesn't really change over time, according to Snidman. The babies who calmly soak up stimulation are likely to continue to do so as adults; the ones who are extremely reactive to stimulation will likely grow up to be shy or socially anxious. This provides evidence for the theory that we're born with a certain temperament, and that temperament follows us into adulthood.

Why does it matter that you were born an introvert and that you'll likely stay an introvert for life? Because you don't want to spend your life pretending to be someone you're not. As an introvert, it's important to recognize that your needs are always going to be slightly different from the needs of extroverts—and learn how to work with your introversion, rather than fight against it.

What Introverts Are Like as Kids

When you ask introverts what they were like as kids, the picture is clear that introversion is something that shows up early on. Jessica, an introvert I interviewed, tells me that she never consistently had large groups of friends. Instead, she liked doing things alone, such as playing with her dollhouse, reading, and playing dress-up. When she did spend time with other children, it was usually in small groups. "I only had one or two close friends for most of my childhood," she says.

Richard was obsessed with books. "I didn't want to be bothered with anyone," he tells me. "I didn't really fit in with folks when I was younger. Nobody really talks to you if you didn't keep up with basketball, go to the same school, or talk about the latest sneakers." Thankfully, things got better as he grew older. "High school was better because I usually hung out with the goths and gamers," he says.

Nicole was the child that no one knew was in the room because she was so quiet. "I almost always played by myself," she says. "I never really was into having friends over or anything like that!" Even as a baby, her parents could put her on a blanket with a few toys and turn their backs. When they came to check on her, "I was still in the same spot, quietly playing alone," she says.

Lori, who is fifty years old, says she is definitely the same as when she was a child. "I was content by myself, even happier that way most of the time," she tells me. "I knew I was different and still do. I love being alone."

Temperaments Don't Change, but Personalities Do

There's another piece to the puzzle of who you are: your personality. Remember: personality and temperament are different. Your personality is shaped by your circumstances and experiences; your temperament is encoded in your DNA from birth. Turns out, both your personality *and* temperament work together to create who you are. It's both nature *and* nurture.

For example, let's say you were an introvert who was lucky enough to grow up in an environment that supported your quiet nature. Parents and teachers praised you for being thoughtful and analytical. They understood your need for alone time and helped you socialize in a way that worked for you. They encouraged you to seek opportunities that played to your strengths, and most important, they didn't make you feel "less than" for not being like the extroverted kids. If they did this, you probably grew up to be a fairly well-adjusted introvert who feels comfortable in your own skin.

Unfortunately, this isn't always the case. Instead of being praised for being thoughtful, many introverts are told they're "too quiet." Parents order them to "stop spending so much time in your room" and teachers tell them to participate more. Introverted kids get the message that there's something wrong with them because they'd rather do an activity quietly and alone rather than hang out with friends every weekend. If this is the kind of childhood you had, you may have grown up to be an adult who feels broken. The good news is it's not too late to change that.

So, when people say that bullying or a nasty breakup transformed them from an extrovert to an introvert, is that right? Not exactly. People are born being more introverted or extroverted, and circumstances won't change that. But here's the catch. Circumstances can change your *personality*. Snidman tells me, "Personality can become modified over time as environmental events occur. Our perceptions of the world and responses to it can change to a greater or lesser extent depending on experiences in our life." Sadly, if you were bullied as a kid or if the love of your life broke up with you, you're going to be negatively impacted. You may become more withdrawn, more cautious, and less confident overall. For a time, you may want to stay home more and interact with fewer people. It may seem like you've suddenly become an introvert. However, it isn't your temperament that has changed—it is a personality shift. This shift could be temporary or last for a while.

Why Your Personality Changes

There's good news about personality changes. According to Christopher Soto, a member of the executive board of the Association for Research in Personality, when people's personalities change over time, it's usually for the better. Several studies, including some of Soto's, show that most adults become more agreeable, conscientious, and emotionally resilient as they get older. These changes don't happen overnight. Rather, they happen gradually, unfolding across years or even decades.

We still don't fully understand all the causes of personality change. However, researchers have identified some potential reasons:

- **Social roles**—Research by Brent Roberts and others shows that the social roles we invest in can change us. In other words, as our lives change, so do our personalities. For example, you may become more conscientious and responsible when you become a parent for the first time. I experienced a slight personality change when I became a teacher. Over time, I became more comfortable with public speaking, being the center of attention, and making small talk. But I didn't become an extrovert. I'm still truly an introvert.

- **Trauma**—Sadly, traumatic events can change your personality, too. As humans, we tend to be more profoundly altered by highly unpleasant experiences than by highly pleasurable ones. In other words, our brains *overlearn* from negative experiences—especially as children. For example, if you were bullied as a child, your personality may have suffered. This is because traumatic experiences can produce changes in the brain. This can lead to shifts in intelligence, emotional reactivity, happiness, sociability, and other traits. The good news is you can actively work to erase some of the effects of trauma; for a great resource on how to do this, check out Rick Hanson's book, *Hardwiring Happiness: The New Brain Science of Contentment, Calm, and Confidence.*

- **Intentional changes**—You may be able to intentionally change your personality through sustained effort and careful goal-setting, according to a 2015 study by Nathan Hudson and Chris Fraley. Other studies by Christopher Soto and Jule Specht suggest that you're more likely to experience positive personality changes if you're leading a meaningful, satisfying life.

Your Introversion Doesn't Have to Doom You

Andre Sólo is an introvert who made intentional personality changes. He grew up a self-professed nerd. You know the type: pimply, clumsy, and one who likes to read lots of sci-fi. Andre wasn't just an introvert; he was awkward, too.

As an adult, he wanted to change his blundering ways. He wondered if there was a way to stop appearing so socially awkward and maybe even enjoy talking to people. So he set out to try. True to nerd form, he started with a spreadsheet. He listed all the changes he wanted to see, the steps it would take to attain them, and a designated challenge to reach each one.

His first challenge was to start conversations with five strangers. But these conversations couldn't be with just anyone—Andre created some rules. Servers didn't count (they're paid to be nice) and a friend-of-a-friend was too easy. And the interaction had to be real, not just, "Hi, how are you?"

Andre's first victim was in an art museum. As she stood quietly contemplating a painting, Andre asked what she thought of it—by practically shouting his question from across the room. To his surprise, she didn't seem annoyed. As she poured her heart out about the painting, Andre mentally made a check mark on his list: one out of five conversations, done! Then he said, "Thanks!" and ran for it. Clearly, he had a long way to go.

These conversations weren't easy. "I didn't want to do them," Andre tells me. "I was completely out of my element." He had to accept the fact that he was going to put himself in a situation where, at some point, he would get embarrassed. "You look like a fool at first," Andre says. "That's the cost of doing it."

But he found that stepping out of his comfort zone was like lifting weights at the gym—it's hard at first, but it gets a little easier each time. His next conversation was with a man in a restaurant. Andre asked him about the book he was reading, and they actually had a little back-and-forth.

Andre went on to improve as a conversationalist. Each day, he chose three topics he could talk about before he left the house. One was "Did you hear about . . . (a recent news story)?"; one was "Did you know that . . . (an interesting new discovery)?"; and one was "What if . . . (an imaginative, fun scenario)?" And, true to the advice found in self-help books, Andre discovered that everyone enjoys talking about themselves. He learned to ask a lot of questions about the other person. He made it a rule that the question "What do you do for a living?" would never be one of them, because he didn't enjoy that kind of small talk.

Today, Andre is a lot better at talking to people, and this has paid off in many ways. His boss and coworkers started to like him more, and he felt more confident striking up conversations with women he wanted to date. Andre made meaningful friendships, too. Soon after improving his conversation skills, he met a new friend in a bar (the kind of place he used to hate going to). She remarked that Andre was one of those special people who was just born with the "gift of gab." When he explained that being charming didn't come naturally to him, she was shocked.

But the best thing to come out of improving his conversation skills wasn't that he could make more friends and go on more dates. "I actually started to enjoy talking with people," he says. "Instead of dreading it, it was fun." Similarly, when a stranger strikes up a conversation with him now, he no longer feels like it's an assault on his private mental state (at least, most of the time).

Andre is still an introvert. Now an author, he spends most of his days writing alone. He dreams up fantastical worlds and makes them come to life through his stories. And he's choosy about the social events he attends.

Andre says it felt good to conquer a weakness of his. "I think this is the best thing introverts can do for themselves," he says. "That, and accept yourself."

If you want to get better at making friends or holding conversations, your introversion doesn't have to doom you. Like Andre, you can learn and practice the skills you need to make these things happen—and reap the benefits as you improve over time.

The Four Types of Introverts

No two introverts are exactly alike. Andre was methodical about improving his social skills (e.g., by using a spreadsheet), but your approach might be different. Similarly, we're all sensitive to different things. Some introverts are extremely bothered by noise and big groups, while for other introverts, crowds aren't a big deal. An hour of socializing might be too much for one introvert, while another can do a few events before feeling drained.

Psychologist Jonathan Cheek, along with graduate students Jennifer Grimes and Courtney Brown, wanted to explore these differences. They hypothesized that there are different types of introverts, or in other words, different ways in which a person's introversion can be expressed. They surveyed about five hundred adults of various ages, asking them about their preferences for spending time alone, how likely they were to daydream, etc. They came up with four types of introverts: social, thinking, anxious, and restrained. They named their model "STAR," after the first letter of each type.

According to their model, a person can be predominately one type (for example, you could be solely a "thinking" introvert). Or you could be a blend of two or more types. Read the following descriptions. Which type (or types) sound like you? Then, if you want to dive deep, take Cheek's STAR quiz in the sidebar.

Social—Don't be fooled. This isn't what it sounds like. A "social" introvert in Cheek's model isn't an introvert who is so outgoing that they can pass for an extrovert. A "social" introvert is someone who is introverted in a social way. It means you have a preference for hanging out with just a few people at a time. Or, sometimes, you prefer not to hang out with anyone at all—people who are high in social introversion like being alone. Instead of partying on a Saturday night, you'd rather stay home and play your favorite video game or watch Netflix. Of course, this assumes that you're staying home because you have a preference for low-key activities, and not because you're shy or have social anxiety. Shyness and social anxiety are not the same as introversion.

Thinking—Like the term sounds, a "thinking" introvert is someone who is introspective, thoughtful, and self-reflective. This person daydreams and enjoys losing themselves in their inner fantasy world. We're not talking about neurotically losing a grip on reality, though; this is about imagination and creativity. Unlike social introverts, thinking introverts don't share the same aversion to social activities that people usually associate with introversion. So, a thinking introvert might hang out with their friends all weekend but then spend Sunday night alone journaling, daydreaming, or working on their graphic novel.

Anxious—While social introverts seek solitude because they prefer low-key activities, anxious introverts avoid socializing because they feel awkward and painfully self-conscious around other people. These are people who are likely not very confident in their social skills. Unfortunately, their anxiety doesn't lessen when they're alone, because this type of introversion is defined by a tendency to ruminate. An anxious introvert may turn things over and over in their mind, wondering what could have, or what already has, gone wrong. They may have trouble shutting off their obsessive negative thoughts. They may even stay awake, late at night, playing events over and over in their mind. That embarrassing thing they said five years ago? It still haunts them today.

Restrained—Do you jump out of bed, ready to seize the day? Do you like to keep busy as much as possible? Is your motto, "I'll try anything once!" If so, you're probably *not* a restrained introvert. Restrained introverts tend to operate at a slightly slower pace. They may take a while to get going. They prefer to think before they speak or act. To relax, they like to slow down and take it easy, as opposed to seeking out new or exciting experiences and sensations. They may sometimes feel sluggish and lacking energy.

The STAR model is a work in progress, and not all introverts fall neatly into its categories. Nevertheless, it's an important step forward in expanding the definition of introversion. Interestingly, Cheek and his colleagues believe that the term *introversion* should never be used by itself. Instead they argue that we should put a specific modifier in front of the word, like "social" or "anxious," for example, by explaining to a curious extrovert: "Yes, I'm an introvert, but I'm a *thinking* introvert, which means large groups don't bother me, but I like having plenty of time alone to think and reflect."

Quiz—Which of the Four Types of Introverts Are You?

To find out where you stand on each of the four meanings of introversion, answer the following questions by deciding to what extent each item is characteristic of your feelings and behavior. Fill in the blank next to each item by choosing a number from the following scale:

1 = very uncharacteristic or untrue, strongly disagree
2 = uncharacteristic
3 = neutral
4 = characteristic
5 = very characteristic or true, strongly agree

Social Introversion

_____ 1. I like to share special occasions with just one person or a few close friends, rather than have big celebrations.

_____ 2. I try to structure my day so that I always have some time to myself.

_____ 3. My ideal vacation involves lots of time to relax by myself.

_____ 4. After spending a few hours surrounded by a lot of people, I am usually eager to get away by myself.

_____ 5. I usually prefer to do things alone.

_____ 6. Other people tend to misunderstand me—forming a mistaken impression of what kind of person I am because I don't say much about myself.

_____ 7. I feel drained after social situations, even when I enjoyed myself.

Thinking Introversion

_____ 1. I enjoy analyzing my own thoughts and ideas about myself.

_____ 2. I have a rich, complex inner life.

_____ 3. I frequently think about what kind of person I am.

_____ 4. When I am reading an interesting story or novel, or when I am watching a good movie, I imagine how I would feel if the events in the story were happening to me.

_____ 5. I generally pay attention to my inner feelings.

_____ 6. I sometimes step back (in my mind) in order to examine myself from a distance.

_____ 7. I daydream and fantasize with some regularity about things that might happen to me.

Anxious Introversion

_____ 1. When I enter a room, I often become self-conscious and feel that the eyes of others are upon me.

_____ 2. My thoughts are often focused on episodes of my life that I wish I'd stop thinking about.

_____ 3. My nervous system sometimes feels so frazzled that I just have to go off by myself.

_____ 4. I don't feel very confident about my social skills.

_____ 5. Defeat or disappointment usually shame or anger me, but I try not to show it.

_____ 6. It takes me some time to overcome my shyness in new situations.

_____ 7. Even when I am in a group of friends, I often feel very alone and uneasy.

Restrained Introversion

_____ 1. I have a hard time getting moving when I wake up in the morning.

_____ 2. For relaxation, I like to slow down and take things easy.

_____ 3. I am often slow to speak, thinking carefully about what I say before I say it.

_____ 4. It's very hard for me to step out of my comfort zone. I rarely seek new experiences and sensations.

_____ 5. Being busy stresses me out.

_____ 6. I need plenty of time to think before I act.

_____ 7. I usually stop and think things over before making a decision.

How Did You Do?

To find out your score, add together all of your answers for each set of seven items to come up with a total score for each kind.

Here's a guide of how you scored compared to others in the general population:

Social Introversion

If you scored below 17, you are low in social introversion. If you scored around 21, you are average in social introversion. If you scored above 25, you are high in social introversion.

Thinking Introversion

Low: below 18
Average: around 21
High: above 24

Anxious Introversion

Low: below 15
Average: around 19
High: above 23

Restrained Introversion

Low: below 15
Average: around 20
High: above 25

Why Introverts Might Struggle to Put Their Thoughts into Words

No matter what type of introvert you are, I bet you've experienced a scenario like this. A coworker barges into your office or a friend puts you on the spot. They ask a question, their tone of voice saying they want an answer *now*. Their request is easy, but your mind feels momentarily paralyzed. You start sentences, then stop them. You say words that are close to what you mean but not exactly. You backtrack. The other person looks at you, almost like they are saying, *Come on, spit it out.* You think, *If only my brain would cooperate.*

Trying to think of exactly the right words to say is called "word retrieval," and it's something many introverts struggle with. In social situations, this may translate to us not being able to keep up with fast-talking extroverts. At work, we may come off sounding like we don't know what we're talking about, even when we do. In the classroom, we may shrink from raising our hand, because we know it will be hard to put our thoughts into words while our classmates stare at us.

One reason word retrieval can be difficult for introverts is we process information deeply. We chew on ideas, turning them over and over in our minds, and often analyzing them from every angle. When you're in "reflecting mode," it's hard to talk. Introverts don't think out loud like many extroverts do; we do our processing inwardly.

Another reason has to do with long-term memory, argues Dr. Marti Olsen Laney in *The Introvert Advantage*. Information stored in long-term memory is mostly outside our conscious awareness. Like the name sounds, long-term memory contains information that is retained for long periods of time; in theory, it's saved indefinitely. Some of this information is fairly easy to access, while other memories are more difficult to recall. For example, do you remember what your first day of kindergarten was like?

Compare this with working memory (sometimes referred to as short-term or active memory), which is limited and retains information for mere seconds. Working memory puts information on the tip of your tongue. It's easy to access, but you don't store the information for long, unless you move it to long-term memory.

Laney suggests that introverts favor long-term memory over working memory. If that's the case, this explains why word retrieval can be difficult for us. It's harder to access the information stored in long-term memory. The right association, or key, is needed to "pull up" the information you're trying to recall—something that reminds you of the stored memory. For example, if you tried to recall your first day of kindergarten, perhaps you looked around the room and noticed a pair of sneakers. This made you remember that someone spilled milk on your shoes on the first day of kindergarten and, *BAM*, suddenly you start remembering more about that day.

And, if you happen to be even the slightest bit anxious when you're trying to speak—like someone putting you on the spot—it may be more difficult to articulate the right words. Not all introverts have social anxiety or are shy, but it's not unusual for an introvert to experience some level of anxiety in a social situation. Anxiety is mentally draining, and can make it harder to recall information. That's because the stress hormone cortisol is released in large amounts during times of anxiety. Cortisol affects the brain and can lead to memory loss and problems with recall.

As an introvert, you may feel that you express yourself best when you can write out your thoughts. For example, you may prefer text messages and emails to phone calls and in-person meetings. Similarly, many introverts journal to process their experiences better. The reason for this preference again has to do with how our brains are wired. According to Laney, you use different brain pathways when writing than when speaking, and these "writing" pathways seem to flow more effortlessly for introverts.

When Your Mind Goes Blank

To yank something out of long-term memory, you need to locate the right association or "key." The good news is most pieces of information in long-term memory were stored with several keys for unlocking them. A key might take the form of a thought, emotion, or sensory association, such as a smell, image, sound, or even a feeling in your body. If you can find just one key, you might be able to pull up the whole memory. Here are some ideas to help you do that:

- Be still and relax.
- Give yourself permission to be quiet for a few moments. Don't let the other person rush you.
- Buy yourself time by saying something like, "Let me think about that," or, "Hmm, let me see . . ." Or, give a nonverbal

signal that shows you're thinking, like looking away and furrowing your brow slightly.

- Let your mind wander, jumping from memory to memory. One thought may lead to another, and one of those thoughts may hold the key to unlocking the words you need.

If all else fails, and words escape you, don't feel embarrassed—your brain is doing what comes naturally to it, and that is to pause and reflect. If you're being quiet, you're in good company with other deep-thinking introverts; the brilliant physicist Stephen Hawking once said, "Quiet people have the loudest minds." Try breezing over any awkwardness by using humor to make light of your tongue-tied state. Or say you're a little distracted right now, but you'll get back to them later—by sending an email or a text.

In Closing

Introverts may not naturally have the "gift of gab" or have as much energy for socializing and meeting new people as extroverts do. But the introvert's mind is a powerful force (we'll explore just how powerful it is later in this book). I hope learning about the science behind introversion has given you an "aha!" moment, like it did for me many years ago—and has helped you understand and appreciate your temperament more.

Chapter 3

INTROVERTS ARE RUDE (AND OTHER MISCONCEPTIONS)

I recently attended a blogging workshop. Seated at a table with three other writers, we introduced ourselves by saying what we wrote about. There was a food writer, a political junkie, and a parenting blogger. Then it was my turn. "I'm Jenn, and I write about introverts," I said, reminding myself to use my "loud-confident" voice while smiling and briefly looking each person in the eye. (Don't laugh. I bet you say things like this in your head, too. Talking to strangers is hard.)

The food blogger perked up. She had been chatting up the table from the moment I sat down. She would later tell me that she identifies as an extrovert. "Oh, that's great!" she cooed. "So you teach introverts *how not to be introverted?*"

I stared at her. A dozen thoughts exploded in my head at once. I wanted to tell her that introverts don't need to be fixed. That there's nothing wrong with being an introvert. I could feel myself tensing up as I opened my mouth to speak.

But I didn't say any of that. I didn't have to. Suddenly, the political junkie chimed in. "I'm an introvert, and I don't want to change that," she proudly declared. "I think you're misunderstanding what it means to be introverted."

I swear I almost shouted, "Amen!"

Unfortunately, this sort of thing happens all the time. Like the extroverted blogger, people have the wrong idea about introversion. Even some *introverts* don't understand it. Once, someone told me they liked spending time alone, were not into big social events, and listened more than they spoke—but there was no way they could be an introvert because they didn't get nervous when talking to people. Similarly, I see a lot of misconceptions about introversion online. Google's definition of an introvert is "a shy, reticent person." (Not all introverts are shy, and I think *reticent* misses the mark.) Even in my own Facebook group for introverts, people confuse introversion with depression, anxiety, or mental illness.

Likewise, while writing this book, I came face-to-face with misconceptions about introversion. When I told others that my book was about introverts, they'd often get a funny look on their face. "Are you an introvert?" they'd usually ask next. It seemed as though they were surprised to find out that a self-professed introvert could even hold a conversation. "Oh, you must feel *waaaaay* out of your comfort zone talking to me then!" one very extroverted woman I had just met exclaimed. (I didn't.) "But you're not an introvert," another said. "I've seen you talk to people!"

And there's another reason to debunk misconceptions about introverts. Research by Aron W. Siegman and Theodore

M. Dembroski suggests that acting falsely extroverted can lead to burnout, stress, and cardiovascular disease. More research into this area is still needed, but this effect is likely caused by the overstimulation and anxiety that can result from introverts overextending themselves socially. Turns out, embracing your introverted nature isn't just a feel-good axiom; it's actually good for your physical health. But we can't embrace our quiet nature until we understand what it truly is—and that starts with clearing up misconceptions about it.

Has someone ever had the wrong idea about you? Read on. In this chapter, we'll address some common misconceptions about introversion.

Misconception #1: Introversion Is Simply Rudeness

It was my first year of college, and the sophomore in the dorm room across the hall from me had invited me to dinner. She was outgoing, loud, and blunt—the kind of person who would say anything to anyone. In hindsight, she was probably an extrovert.

At the restaurant, we ordered appetizers, and she asked me where I was from (Minnesota) and what my major was (writing)—all the usual get-to-know-you small talk. I thought our first "friend date" was going well, as well as it could for a socially awkward introvert like me. But then she said something that shocked me. "You're actually a really cool person. When I first met you, you hardly said anything, so I thought you were kind of a bitch."

Kind of a bitch. She tossed off the words as coolly as if she had just informed me that my mozzarella sticks had arrived. In some twisted way, I think she meant it as a compliment.

I didn't know what to say. I froze, then uttered a weak "Haha, thanks." I tried to pretend like everything was okay, but in reality, her words wounded me. Sure, I was quiet. I kept to myself on campus. I often spent Friday nights lying in bed reading books from my classes that I found interesting. I had a boyfriend and a few close friends, and they were all I needed to fill my social quota. I'd never thought my introverted ways were seen as bitchy. I was just doing my own thing.

Turns out, being called bitchy, rude, or aloof is a common introvert problem. "I have been accused of being an arrogant prick for avoiding small talk and favoring solitude," Leylani tells me. "I've been called 'ice queen,'" Anne says. "Also, many people have told me, 'You scared me when I first met you' because I didn't smile all the time." Allison adds, "After high school, when I would happen to meet someone I hadn't seen since high school, it inevitably would be said that they thought I was stuck up or bitchy." She would ask them if she had ever said something rude to them. "And it would turn out that, no, I didn't, but because I often sat alone and read or had headphones on, people assumed I thought I was superior to them. That baffled me. I certainly didn't want to be in with the 'in' crowd, but I also didn't actively dislike most people. Mostly I was just busy with my books and music and such."

To this day, I can't think of a time when I had been outright rude to my dormmate. I'd never insulted her, walked away when she was talking, or anything of the sort. What had probably happened was I'd passed her several times in the hallway, before we were friends, and hadn't said much. I definitely didn't stick my hand out and exclaim, "Hi, I'm Jenn! How's your day going?" I didn't see this as being rude. I was simply keeping to myself.

And herein lies the problem. Our reserved nature gets us in trouble. We don't bubble over with pleasantries, so we get accused of being unfriendly. We don't blab our life story to people we've just met, so we get accused of being aloof. But introverts don't see life as one big cocktail party. We're content with just a few meaningful relationships. We're not constantly scanning the environment, looking to add more adoring fans to our entourage.

As we go through the day, we're likely in our heads. Shalima, another introvert who has been accused of being rude, tells me, "When your mind is screaming at you with thoughts and ideas coming at you all at once, it's hard to be loud." Or we're simply observing our surroundings, as introverts tend to do. Amy says, "Quiet doesn't equal mad, sad, rude, bitchy, arrogant, or stuck-up. Quiet *does* equal people-watching, observing, and enjoying life . . . quietly."

When my extroverted dormmate called me a bitch, I wish I'd spoken up. I wish I would have told her not to make assumptions about someone who is quiet. A person can be quiet for many reasons. They might be an introvert who needs time to warm up to new people. They might be turned inward at the moment, enjoying the thoughts in their private inner world. Or that quiet person may simply be content with silence. Don't be too quick to judge.

Today, I make a point of saying hello when I pass neighbors in the hallway of my apartment building. When I'm in the right mood, I even engage in some back-and-forth ("Hey, I like your coat! Where'd you get it?"). But I probably won't hang around having a fifteen-minute conversation that started with "How 'bout this weather?" (Unless it's snowing, of course, which in that case is the *only* thing we Minnesotans want to talk about.) And I probably won't spontaneously invite anyone in for tea. I'm okay with that.

Misconception #2: The Introvert's Need for Solitude Is Antisocial

When Jill was in high school, she felt exhausted and drained all the time because she didn't know how to work with her introversion like she does now. As a result, she got in a lot of trouble with her parents. "They never seemed to understand why I wanted to be on my own all the time, and I'm pretty sure they worried I was depressed or into something I shouldn't have been into since I liked to just sit at the computer all night," she tells me. "Thus, I was 'antisocial' and 'had a problem.'" It got to the point where Jill couldn't even handle the social stimulation from being in class. "I completely shut down and tuned out during the day at school," she says. "My teachers sat me down with my parents and basically told me to participate *or else*. I felt like I was defective, or a bad kid. I was just waiting for them to send me off to therapy or something so I could be 'fixed' for not wanting to participate."

Now Jill knows she felt drained because she was overstimulated from being around people and not being able to fully recharge afterward. "There was always so much pressure to participate in clubs, and then friends wanted a lot of my attention, too, once we got out of class," she tells me. "If I didn't give it to them, that caused a whole other slew of problems because if I wasn't 100 percent devoted to them, I was a 'bad friend.' I basically had to fake being an extrovert to get through it, and as a result, I was crabby and a 'stuck-up bitch'—this was a direct quote from an old classmate."

Connie had a similar problem. "I have a 'good friend' whom I will call Nikki," she says. "She is incredibly extroverted, funny, creative, well-spoken, and caring, but *loud.* She is loud *in every single way.* She talks loudly, she mothers loudly, she creates loudly, and in her relationships, she needs loud face-to-face time. She needs that intense, outside stimulation. So when we became what she considered to be close friends, she took to calling me antisocial at every opportunity, due to the fact that I don't share her need for outside stimulation."

According to Connie, Nikki is a psychology major, so she feels like she "gets" everyone. "Maybe she understands that people have differing personalities and quirks, but as far as truly understanding, I beg to differ," Connie says. "She would tease me about not wanting to go out with her and her friends and for having a clean home and an orderly life—from her perspective." Connie thinks this is due to them having opposite personalities. "Just ten minutes with Nikki and I would start to check out. I would become completely overstimulated by all her loudness and her need to dominate the conversation. Hey, I'm as introverted as they come, but I do enjoy contributing to the conversation once in a while. Introversion does not equate to being antisocial, though I used to think so. That is until I truly came to understand and accept myself as an introvert."

Jill and Connie are the victims of another nasty misconception about introversion: Our need for alone time is seen as unsociable. Unhealthy, even. Extroverts can't fathom why we want to be alone often—they figure there's no way it can be good for us.

What they don't understand is there's a tiny, invisible battery inside introverts. This metaphorical battery contains all our juice for social interaction. When a chatty coworker goes on and on about her weekend and you're forced to listen, your battery drains a little. When you do a group lunch with everyone in your office and polite chitchat is mandatory, your battery drains more. When you attend your second cousin's wedding and play nice with relatives who last saw you when you were "only this tall!" your battery becomes depleted. It's not that introverts have an unhealthy need to be alone. Solitude is our sanity.

In Their Own Words

I asked introverts to tell me about the misconceptions they face that are related to their introversion. Here's what they said:

> "A misconception about us that I've run into is even after you explain what introversion is, a lot of times an extrovert still tries to give you advice on how to be more extroverted. What's frustrating is that this implies that introversion is an inferior personality type. It's like they think introverts just need to

hear how to be extroverts, as if haven't been told that our entire lives. This is frustrating, but I think introverts have a responsibility to show the world that the way we approach the world is valid and doesn't need to be fixed."

—Shelby

"I think the biggest misconception is that all introverts have social anxiety and don't enjoy socializing. My extroverted coworker knows that I'm an introvert. There have been times when she's assumed that I wouldn't be interested in things that involve socializing or presenting because I'm an introvert. If I mention I went to a party or something over the weekend, she will respond, 'Are you sure you're an introvert?' I've explained that being an introvert doesn't mean that I dislike people or socializing or that I'm shy, just that I need more alone time to recharge my batteries."

—Megan

"When I was explaining introversion to someone, they asked, 'Aren't you on medication for that?' I asked what medication and they said, 'Oh, you know, antidepressants.'"

—Chuk

"I once had an extroverted roommate who could never understand the hour of quiet, alone time

I needed after work to decompress from taking phone calls all day. I told her I was going into my room and shutting the door, and that no, I wasn't mad at her, and no, I wasn't depressed. I just needed some alone time. Almost every day she would knock on my door, then open it. 'Are you mad at me? What's wrong? Let's go out!' Argh! I had to ask her to move out after a couple of months. She just didn't get it, and she told all of our mutual friends how stuck up and moody I was."

—Amy

"I am a teacher and I know how to turn myself on to teach and interact and lead others, but then I need to turn off to recharge. Once I was introduced to a group of my peers that I was about to present a training to—as 'a shy person.' I hated being called shy because I am not shy. I just prefer to not speak if I have nothing to say."

—Jennifer

"It's been my experience that people have often thought that I'm not as intelligent as I am. They assumed because I didn't contribute to the conversation, and chose instead to listen and observe, that I was dumb."

—Bonnie

"The biggest misconception I've faced as an introvert is that people think I'm not one! Most people in my life really struggle to understand that I have a lot of social anxiety, and it actually makes me 'perform' in public like I'm extroverted. I can be chatty, loud, engaged . . . but all of it comes from fear, anxiety, and pressure. When I'm really being myself, I'm actually very quiet and reserved."

—Aidan

"We don't hate people. We just like to save our energy for certain things, and shallow interaction doesn't cut it. But we are capable of small talk, though I can list about a thousand other things I would rather be doing."

—Kamiko

"I don't like the misunderstanding that introverts are necessarily hermits. We are human and have social needs as well."

—Nelia

"People say, 'There's no way you're an introvert, you're so good at talking to people!' I've worked in many jobs where I have to be 'on' most of the time. Because of this, I know how to do small talk and can do it well. But others don't see what happens when I get home. I have to totally shut down, sometimes for up to an hour, to recharge enough to do tasks at home. It has taken me quite some time to realize that just because I'm able to chat doesn't mean I'm an extrovert (like people told me), and to realize I need alone time to recharge. Now that I know this, I can begin to change my work habits and have a healthy inner life."

—Rebecca

"The problem I run into frequently is the lunch break scenario. I like people and make friends easily, but I don't like mindless socializing. Consequently, I prefer to eat lunch on my own. I find the noisy chitchat exhausting, and I need my lunch break time to clear my mind for the afternoon's work. Most of my colleagues understand, but there are some who just don't get it!"

—Lawrence

"People constantly underestimate me because I'm quiet and I don't talk a lot. They don't realize I like to stay out of the limelight and observe. I like to work behind the scenes and fly under the radar. I know so much more than they think I know, and I prefer it that way."

—Emily

> "I think the worst part of growing up introverted was that people assumed I wanted to be otherwise. If you sit in a tree with a book at recess people assume you wish you were braiding hair with the pretty girls or smoking pot with the badass kids, but really you're happy with what you're doing."
>
> —Allison

Misconception #3: Introverts Lack Passion

People often accuse Leanne Chapman of being unemotional. In an *Introvert, Dear* article, she writes, "Have you ever been to a workshop where the speaker bounds onto the stage and shouts, 'ARE YOU EXCITED?!' Or maybe someone gleefully asks you the same question at a party or social gathering. If you're an introvert like me, you might find this question daunting. I can be excited about something but I won't show it outwardly—although the people who know me well can tell. I'm introspective and quiet by nature, so my response to the question can simply be 'Yes,' said with a smile."

I can relate to Leanne's problem. There have been many times in my life when my lack of outward enthusiasm has created issues. For example, a few years ago, when I was dating for the first time as an adult, guys would tell me they thought I didn't like them. Sometimes they were right—after a first date, I wanted nothing to do with them. But other times, I'd be swooning and planning our future together as Paramore's "The Only Exception" played in my head. But I didn't show my feelings in the typical extroverted way. I didn't gush, sigh, or giggle. In fact, it seemed like the more I was into someone, the more I clammed up. Talk about counterproductive.

Although Leanne and I would probably get cut from the pep squad, that doesn't mean we lack passion. Just because we don't look excited doesn't mean we're not into something. Introverts can be just as emotional as extroverts—but we usually keep the bulk of those feelings hidden inside. Even if we're having a bad day and a coworker asks, "How are you?" we may not want to talk about it. As Michaela Chung, author of *The Irresistible Introvert* puts it, "That's the thing about introverts; we wear our chaos on the inside where no one can see it." At least until you get to know us really, *really* well.

Eventually, Leanne learned to not care about what other people thought of her lack of enthusiasm. "If anyone says I don't look excited enough or I'm too quiet, I will smile and point out that it's just my nature," she writes. "I don't feel the need to defend myself, or to spend a lot of time with those people, because it doesn't do me any good to be around anyone who inadvertently triggers my old beliefs about myself."

"What many fail to see is that deep within the introvert there is a lot going on," she continues. "But rather than giving it a voice directly through talk and chatter, the introvert expresses it through activism, journaling, painting, creating music, planting a flower garden, fighting for some special cause, or even well-placed silence."

Misconception #4: Introverts Hate People

In his semiautobiographical screenplay *Barfly*, Charles Bukowski penned a line that, decades later, would go on to become the introvert's anthem. This line gets passed around a lot in introvert circles—perhaps you've heard it. In the screenplay, Wanda, a woman who has shacked up with the main character, Henry, asks him if he hates people. Henry, a lonely alcoholic, answers that no, despite appearances, he doesn't; he simply feels better when there aren't any people around. Unfortunately, like Henry, many introverts get accused of being misanthropes. Our friends and loved ones think we dislike people because we like spending time alone. However, for most introverts, this is simply not true. In fact, some introverts like people so much that they've chosen "extroverted" careers that force them to interact with people every day. Their jobs drain them, but they feel the sacrifice is worth it in order to serve humankind. Many introverts are social workers, teachers, counselors, doctors, project managers, and so on. For example, Karen has been an IT project manager in the health-care industry for over thirty-five years. She tells me that what she likes the most about her job is being able to help people use technology. There's also Vanessa, who has been a social worker for ten years. She likes that her job lets her really get to know people and hear their stories. She gets to skip the small talk and jump right into meaningful conversation. Finally, Mary, a manufacturing consultant, feels that helping people by sharing her gifts is worth the sacrifice of becoming overstimulated. She says she loves seeing clients grow their businesses and fulfill their dreams.

Misconception #5: All Introverts Are Shy

Another misconception about introverts is that we're all shy. But that's simply not true. Introversion and shyness are two different things. If you're shy, you fear being judged negatively by others; you may frequently feel bashful, timid, nervous, and insecure in social settings, as well as experience physical sensations, such as blushing or feeling shaky and breathless. If you're an introvert, you simply prefer calm, low-key environments. For example, a shy person might skip a dinner party because the thought of making small talk with strangers makes them scared and anxious, while an introvert might skip the party because relaxing at home is more enjoyable.

You can be an introvert who is not shy or an extrovert who is shy. For example, Bill Gates, the co-founder of Microsoft, is an introvert who's not the least bit shy. He's described by Susan Cain in a *Psychology Today* blog post as nerdy and quiet but also unruffled by anyone's opinion of him. On the other hand, Barbra Streisand, the larger-than-life music icon, is likely a shy extrovert. Most people don't know that she struggles with stage fright. After panicking during a performance in Central Park in 1967 and forgetting the words to one of her songs, Streisand avoided live performances for decades.

Of course, you can be both shy and an introvert. As one might predict, psychologists have found that shyness and introversion overlap somewhat, meaning that some introverts act shy and that some shy people are introverted. There are several possible reasons behind this. One reason is some people are born with "high-reactive" temperaments that make them inclined to both shyness and introversion, according to Cain. Also, shy people may become more introverted over time; because social life is a source of anxiety, they may be inspired to discover the joy of being alone. Also, introverts may become shy after repeatedly receiving the message from peers, teachers, and parents that there's something wrong with them.

It's important to know the difference between shyness and introversion, because if you're painfully shy, you can work to overcome your shyness. I did. I grew up horribly shy, but these days, I worry a lot less about what people think of me—and it's freeing. But the more significant takeaway is that there's a bias in our society against both traits. According to Cain, studies show that we rank fast and frequent talkers as more likable, capable, and intelligent than slow, quiet ones. This is the real misconception that needs to be squashed. Just because someone is shy (or introverted) does not mean they are any less competent and smart.

Misconception #6: Introverts Make Poor Leaders

Managing others. Being in the spotlight. Taking risks. These are qualities we associate with leaders—and with extroversion. Does this mean introverts make poor leaders? Not at all. Introverts play a crucial role in every sphere of society, from business to politics to technology. In fact, *USA TODAY* reported that 40 percent of top executives are introverts. And some of the most notable leaders of our time are introverts, such as Bill Gates. He believes that introverts can make strong leaders. Speaking at an engagement in 2013, he said that there's a benefit to being introverted—introverts have the unique ability to separate themselves from others for a few days, which allows them to think deeply about a problem, read everything they can about it, and consider angles that others haven't.

Another introverted leader is Marissa Mayer, the CEO of Yahoo. Mayer told *Vogue* magazine that she gets the urge to run and hide during parties, even parties held at her own house. Her secret to dealing with her social avoidance tendencies? She looks at her watch and tells herself that she can't leave until a certain time. And, she promises herself, if she's still having a terrible time at X, she can leave. However, she usually finds that if she makes herself stay for a certain length of time, she gets over her social awkwardness and ends up having fun.

Finally, there's Barack Obama, the former US president. According to the *New York Times* author Michael D. Shear, Obama spent four or five hours alone almost every night of his presidency. After having dinner with his wife and daughters, he withdrew to his private office, where he worked on speeches, read stacks of briefing papers, and read letters from Americans. But it wasn't all work: Obama indulged in his own version of introvert recharge time by watching ESPN, reading novels, or playing Words With Friends on his iPad. Like other introverts who have been accused of being stuck-up or rude, Obama, too, was criticized for his aloof personality. But it was also his introspective nature and capacity for communication that made him a powerful leader—and that gave him the reputation for having a different style than many on Capitol Hill.

Misconception #7: Introverts Don't Know How to Have Fun

Virginia Miel lives in Mexico, where big and frequent get-togethers are the norm. A quiet introvert, Virginia is often accused by family and friends of not knowing how to have fun. When a friend announced an upcoming birthday party, Virginia swore that this time would be different. She hated how she always became bored, tired, and irritable at parties. "It was a reminder that being me was 'wrong' and that my level of fun was practically nil," she writes in an *Introvert, Dear* article.

But this time, she would be ready. "It took me a whole week to prepare for the party," she writes. "I did Internet research on different ways to start a conversation. I imagined myself dancing around, talking to strangers, and laughing loudly. I swore I would make myself have fun and be like the rest. I was going to *enjoy* this freaking event."

When the day of the party arrived, everyone was in their element, but once again, Virginia found herself shrinking back to a corner of the living room. Later in the night, a friend who always seemed to delight in alienating Virginia approached her. "She pointed out to as many people as possible that I wasn't enjoying myself," Virginia writes. "I responded that I was but that I don't enjoy places with this much noise." Immediately, she regretted saying those words, because they weren't really true—she wasn't having fun and it was obvious. Her "friend" remarked cattily that *she* knew how to have a good time. "When I get older," the friend said, twisting the knife, "I want to remember that I knew how to have fun when I was young."

Virginia suffers from a common introvert misconception. Extroverts think that if something is fun for them, it should be fun for us, too. Although introverts can and do enjoy the occasional party, we generally have a different definition of fun. Our ideal Saturday night probably involves staying home, snuggled in our pajamas, and watching Netflix while eating takeout. Or maybe online gaming, reading a book, working on our graphic novel, coloring, or composing songs. Or getting dinner with one of our favorite friends and talking about everything that is on our minds.

Virginia doesn't worry anymore about what people think of her "boring" ways. "I can be as fun as any other person, but in a different way," she writes. "I love Saturday nights at home. Even if someone invites me to the most amazing party, I will thank that person for the invitation but probably decline. And yes, that's okay."

In Closing

I hope you now have a better idea of what introversion is—and perhaps, more important, what it's not. If someone is surprised to learn that you're an introvert, it could be because they don't understand what introversion truly is. Fight those misconceptions. Introverts are not disturbed recluses who hide away in dark bedrooms. Introverts have fun, laugh, and love, too.

Chapter 4

YES, THE "INTROVERT HANGOVER" IS REAL

Everyone wanted to talk to Shawna Courter. The newest addition to her fiancé's family, she was introduced to what felt like hundreds of people, one after the other, in quick succession. As the night wore on, the people around her became louder and more energetic, but Shawna, an introvert, became so exhausted that she could no longer keep a smile on her face. She couldn't take it anymore. "I slipped away like a thief, skulking about the house, searching for a place where it was quiet," she writes in an *Introvert, Dear* article. Eventually, she found that place: a half-lit room, empty except for her future brother-in-law who was sitting alone, staring out the window.

Knowing he was an introvert, too, Shawna figured this was her best option for escape. She sat down on the opposite side of the room, wrapping her arms around her knees. "I remember hoping he wouldn't think I was intruding upon his own solitude before I allowed myself to zone out, letting my thoughts drown out the raucous laughter from downstairs, breathing deeply and feeling the tension drain away," she writes. "I don't know how long it was before my now-husband came looking for me, but I remember him laughing at finding the two introverts seeking refuge together."

To this day, Shawna and her brother-in-law have not spoken of that night. There's no need, Shawna figures, because they both inherently understood what the other was experiencing: an "introvert hangover" brought on by too much socializing.

"I Become Physically Unwell if I Overextend"

When Shawna wrote about her experience in an article for *Introvert, Dear* called "Yes, There Is Such a Thing as an 'Introvert' Hangover," it went practically viral. Major media outlets like *Inc.* magazine and *New York* magazine chimed in, commenting on hangover "symptoms" and exploring the triggers behind this phenomenon. In the latter publication, Jesse Singal describes his version of the introvert hangover in an article in the *Science of Us* section titled "Introvert Hangovers Can Be Really Rough":

> [It's] more about a general sense of anxiety and impatience. I find it harder and harder to make small talk, and more and more driven to be alone. The mind shutdown resonated, too—it gets harder and harder to fake genuine social interaction (though more so at a party with people I don't know than when in a small group of people I know and like).

It wasn't just other writers who weighed in. The comments section of Shawna's article blew up. "I might need a whole day to myself to recharge after a party, and I really feel like I was hung over: headache, nausea, fatigue, the whole shebang," one reader comments. Another agrees: "I often need the next day to recover, which is why I try really hard to never schedule two days of socializing back to back." And: "I definitely become physically unwell if I overextend."

When Shawna wrote about her experiences, she had no idea she would hit on a topic that resonated so deeply with many introverts. It turns out Shawna was not alone in her introvert hangover. The introvert hangover is real.

What an Introvert Hangover Feels Like

The introvert hangover could also be called "social burnout" or a "social hangover." No matter what we call it, an introvert hangover can be rough. Some introverts experience physical symptoms. For Shawna, "It starts with an actual physical reaction to overstimulation. Your ears might ring, your eyes start to blur, and you feel like you're going to hyperventilate. Maybe your palms sweat."

Also, you may become irritable. This is what happened to Kayla after she spent the day at the Universal Studios theme park with her soon-to-be husband and his family. Even though the outing was fun, she quickly developed an introvert hangover. "I got tired, not just physically tired, but mentally tired, and I got grumpy," she tells me. "You know how a little kid gets fussy when they need a nap? It's the same for me. I needed a mental nap!"

On top of that, your mind may shut down. This happens to Brenda Knowles, an introvert blogger. On her blog *Space2live* found at BrendaKnowles.com, in a post called "Introvert Explained: Why We Love You But Need to Get Away From You," she writes that introverts "are not all recluses hanging out in dusty homes with cats and classic books (not that there's anything wrong with cats and classic books)." Introverts "get out and rock it," but then we need to withdraw. "If we don't, we will feel like an overdone steak—no life, no juice. Our minds will be zapped and cottony. Our speech may come out slowly with pauses between words. There may be tears or swearing, or both."

Most important, when you experience an introvert hangover, you get an overwhelming desire to be alone. "Contrary to popular belief, we introverts do enjoy socializing," writes Michaela Chung, creator of the blog *Introvert Spring*. In a post called "Introvert: How to Cure a Social Hangover," she writes, "We have our playmates and our passions just as extroverts do. Some of us like to dance. Some of us like to drink. Some of us like to flirt, and laugh, and chase sunsets. Some of us have a habit of cramming all of the above into one day. And then, of course, we pay." When this happens, "you don't want to talk to anyone. You just want to close the door and be alone for a while. Not for too long—just until the season turns, or reality TV goes out of style."

Every introvert experiences the introvert hangover a little differently. You may not get sweaty palms like Shawna or feel grouchy like Kayla. You may get an introvert hangover after twenty minutes of socializing or after two days, and it may last for a few minutes or a few hours. Your symptoms and the duration of the hangover will depend on several factors: the social situation itself, your own level of introversion, how much energy you had going into the social event, and the quality of your downtime afterward.

What Everyone Else Does

Unfortunately, when you have an introvert hangover, your problems don't stop at mental and physical exhaustion. When other people notice you're getting burned out, they often make the situation worse, not better. They ask, "Are you feeling okay?" or "Why are you being so quiet?" They have good intentions; they want you to have a good time at the party or get-together, and they're worrying that you're not. What they don't know is being called out doesn't help. In fact, it probably just makes you feel self-conscious, which likely results in you doubling down on your "extroverted" efforts. This expends more social energy and ultimately makes your hangover worse.

Worse yet, people accuse you of being a boring party pooper. "Come on, just relax and have a good time." Or, "Don't you know how to have fun?"

An introvert hangover happens because introverts have a less active dopamine reward system than extroverts, as you learned in Chapter 2. If your friends knew you're an introvert who feels drained by socializing, they would probably understand; they might even help you find a quiet place to recharge or not make you feel guilty for wanting to leave early. The problem is, when you're experiencing an introvert hangover, your feelings seem irrational. Everyone around you is having fun—*they're* not showing signs of social burnout, so why are *you*?

Another problem is, when you feel exhausted and grouchy, the last thing you want is to summon what's left of your energy to give a lengthy explanation. Sure, other people would benefit from knowing about introverts and dopamine, but who wants to give a science lecture when your head is spinning? So you keep your feelings to yourself and end up snapping at others or glowering. You're accused of being no fun. Worst of all, you feel exhausted and unwell.

For Extroverts: Recognizing the Signs of an Introvert Hangover

If you have an introvert in your life, it's important to know the signs of an introvert hangover. Every introvert experiences social burnout in a different way, so they may have symptoms like these, or different ones. Here are general signs to watch for:

- Zoning out, daydreaming, or glazing over
- Becoming quiet
- Irritability, crankiness, grumpiness
- Speaking more slowly and having long pauses between words
- Appearing tired or low in energy
- Getting flustered when having to make decisions
- Feeling physically unwell
- Feeling anxious, down, or depressed
- Wanting to withdraw and be alone

Introverts tend to be highly self-aware, but surprisingly, this doesn't always translate to being aware of our own feelings and bodily sensations. Sometimes *we* don't recognize when we're getting burned out. Seemingly out of nowhere, we become combative, lethargic, and indecisive. Especially if we're used to overextending ourselves, an introvert hangover may just be our norm. You can do your introvert a favor by noticing when they're getting burned out. Check in with them and see if they need to get away and be alone. Your introvert will appreciate that you're looking out for them.

The Only Way to Cure an Introvert Hangover

There's only one cure for the introvert hangover. It's the same cure prescribed for actual hangovers induced by alcohol. No, I'm not talking about taking aspirin or eating a greasy burger (but hey, if it soothes your soul, then why not?). The cure I'm talking about is *time*. In the case of the introvert hangover, it's *time spent alone.*

When it comes to solitude, every introvert has a prescription that works for them. Jonathan Rauch, author of the popular *Atlantic* article, "Caring for Your Introvert," has his need boiled down to a precise formula. After an hour or two of being "on" socially, he finds himself fading. That's when he needs to get away from the crowd and recharge. Roughly, for every one hour spent with people, he spends two hours in solitude. To him, this isn't a symptom of depression or "antisocial" behavior. Rather, being alone feeds him on a mental and emotional level, just like eating and resting sustain the body in a physical way.

Not all alone time is the same. You can be "alone" while answering emails in your private office or driving by yourself in rush hour traffic. Your environment may not even be quiet. But this type of alone time probably won't restore your energy. Although there is no one else around, you're not really relaxed. True restorative alone time allows your mind to wander. You stop paying attention to things in the outside world and instead turn inward. You don't think about what's coming next on your schedule or what other people want you to do. You do whatever you want in the moment, whether it's watching a show on Netflix, listening to music, or reading.

Remember Kayla, the introvert who spent the day at Universal Studios with her soon-to-be in-laws? Although she had an introvert hangover, she couldn't leave the park until the outing was over because the whole family had come together. At one point, when she felt really overloaded, she did something that likely saved the day—she went off on her own for a while. Thankfully, her fiancé (now husband) is an introvert too, so he understood.

One more thing. Alone time doesn't have to be spent completely alone. As Kayla walked through the park, there were swarms of people around her. Nevertheless, she received an energy boost because she got to spend time not *interacting* with anyone. Similarly, for many introverts, downtime with their significant other counts as being "alone." This is time when you're just hanging out and relaxing, with no real demands on you to act a certain way. You might lounge around the house in your pajamas or read a book on the couch while your significant other sits nearby, playing a video game. Though you're not talking, you're in each other's presence. You're being "alone together." This can be just as restorative as actually being by yourself.

Being Alone Can Be Glorious

When you have an introvert hangover, finally getting to be alone is a glorious thing. It's quiet! No small talk! No one is demanding anything from you! When I was a teacher, I relished the moments of quiet at the end of the school day when I could finally close my classroom door and be alone. It was even better when I didn't have any plans after school and could go straight home to an empty apartment. On days when I was really overloaded, I would lie on the couch, just staring off into space. Watching Netflix, reading, or listening to a podcast would have been too much mental stimulation at that point. I needed to just *be*.

One of my most vivid memories of being alone was in college. I had signed up to study abroad in Spain for a semester. As a shy introvert who at the time had never lived anywhere else but Minnesota, this was a big step for me. The first two days of the trip were grueling. Traveling from St. Paul to Madrid, I was surrounded by new people twenty-four seven. What made it worse was everyone seemed to become friends with each other instantly—even though they had never met before. While I was trying to soothe my feelings of overstimulation, they were laughing and having fun. I felt simultaneously bombarded by people *and* left out.

When we finally arrived at our hotel, my classmates quickly put together a plan to go bar hopping. One of them invited me. *Here was my chance*, I thought. *I could finally break into their friend group!* But that thought was quickly replaced with another. I was so exhausted I could barely think straight. I was overwhelmed by so many new things —new people, new food, a new language, and new experiences. I became anxious at the thought of adding one more thing to my already overloaded system.

I didn't go. I just didn't have it in me. I knew staying in meant missing an opportunity to make friends. It also meant I'd have to wait to explore a new city. But I made up my mind that I would have to live with those facts. So I crept back to the hotel room I was sharing with two other women. I crawled into bed, but I didn't fall asleep. Instead, I lay there, relishing the silence and the fact that I was finally alone. Slowly, I could feel my body coming back to life. My mind relaxed, and I started to process all the new things I'd experienced. It was like my thoughts, which had been stuffed away in a jar those last two days, were suddenly released as the jar opened. As my thoughts flew out, I finally made sense of them.

I'd like to say I didn't feel any regret when I saw my class-mates the next day, but that wouldn't be true. They were worn out, but they looked closer than ever. They kept referencing things that had happened the night before, and I had no idea what they were talking about. I was left out of their inside jokes. As the trip went on, I never really made it into their inner circle. But ultimately, I believe I did the right thing. Looking back, high-energy people who partied often probably wouldn't have been the right friend "fit" for this low-key introvert, anyway. Plus, the next day, as we toured an art museum, a church, and other places, I actually had the energy to enjoy these experiences.

When the Choice of Solitude Isn't Clear

Introverts have to make difficult choices all the time like the one I made in Madrid. Should we snatch up an opportunity to experience something new, potentially have fun, and make social connections—even though the trade-off is exhaustion and overstimulation? Or should we stay home and protect our energy, but risk missing out? Sometimes the answer isn't clear.

Rachel Ginder is another introvert who had to make a tough decision. During a trip to Europe with about two dozen other twenty-something-year-olds, the group stopped in Germany for Oktoberfest, one of the world's craziest and most renowned parties. As Rachel headed to the festival, she started to worry. She was someone who rarely got tipsy even at home, and her idea of fun was relaxing quietly with a book. But she told herself she was overreacting. She was young and on the trip of a lifetime. Plus, she had forked over a good chunk of her hard-earned savings to be here. She shouldn't let it go to waste.

As she joined the crushing crowd of Oktoberfest partiers, Rachel felt herself kicking into sensory overload. "The noise was deafening, and I had to nearly scream into the ear of my friend next to me to be heard," she writes in an *Introvert, Dear* article. "I clung to the sleeve of her shirt so we wouldn't be separated in the throng of people, but I found it nearly impossible to keep my grip as I was jostled on all sides."

It took what felt like hours for Rachel to make it several hundred feet to the closest beer tent. "Even after shoving our way inside where the throng was slightly less dense, I felt agitated, shaky, and a little bit dizzy," she writes. "These were not happy adrenaline-fueled responses." Her gut was telling her to leave.

Rachel had a difficult decision to make. Should she give up on this experience of a lifetime? Or should she tough it out in the hope that she'd eventually have fun? After all, she had *chosen* to come on this trip. She was looking for a little excitement.

In the end, Rachel decided to leave. Another introvert in her group who was also not having fun left with her. Rachel didn't even know the person's name until later that night, but in the chaos of Oktoberfest, their social exhaustion united them. They worked together to find the nearest exit and found their way back to their rooms.

At the hotel, Rachel felt better. However, she also realized that leaving Oktoberfest came with a trade-off. "I would like to tell you I felt empowered by my decision, got a full eight hours of sleep, and had no regrets about my choice for the rest of the trip. Unfortunately, that's not wholly the truth," she writes. "The next morning, my friends were full of stories about dancing on tables and meeting cute guys from foreign countries. Once again, I felt an inner war between the part of me that wishes to be spontaneous and the part that knows that just being in another country was already far beyond my usual comfort zone."

Ultimately, Rachel believes she made the right decision. "For me, it's a big deal to make it through a trip without giving in to exhaustion. In order to make it, I need to say no to certain activities to conserve my mental health, even if part of me wants to say yes just for the experience," she writes. "The struggle might be mental rather than physical, but for me it's no different than refusing a piece of cake that might give me a stomachache, or a liter of Oktoberfest beer that might induce a hangover. No one would judge a person for making decisions based on their physical health, so please don't judge me for attempting to maintain my mental health."

Unfortunately, there aren't any hard-and-fast rules for maintaining your mental health like there are for, say, healthy eating or exercise. Everyone needs to figure out what works for them based on their own levels of introversion or extroversion. "One person's party might be another person's worst nightmare," Rachel writes. "The key is not trying to be wild and spontaneous as someone else understands it, but being wild and spontaneous for who you are as an individual. I'm still finding that balance. The more I test my comfort zone, the closer I come to finding where my boundaries lie. Perhaps next time I might consider dancing on a few tables. Or maybe I'll just dance at home by myself, where the lighting is perfect and the music is at just the right level."

Should I Stay or Should I Go?

Like Rachel's experience in Germany and mine in Spain, the choice between staying in and going out isn't always obvious. Maybe you're not on a once-in-a-lifetime trip but are simply trying to decide whether you should attend a friend's birthday party. You don't want to let your friend down. What if the night ends up being fun, and you miss it? However, if you go, you'll likely become exhausted and overstimulated. Often, we don't really know how an event will affect us until we're there.

My personal rule is if I think I'll be able to tolerate the social drain *and* there seems to be a potential for meaningful interaction, I'll go. If I'm already exhausted—because it's been a long work week or I've already had too many social obligations—I skip it. If the event doesn't promise meaningful interaction, that's another reason to stay home. All of this assumes that it wouldn't be incredibly rude of me to decline, meaning it's not my grandpa's ninetieth birthday party or my best friend's wedding. In cases like those, you probably have to suck it up and make an appearance.

It's not always easy to determine if a get-together promises meaningful interaction. Once, I went to a friend's birthday party that involved a huge group dinner followed by hanging out at a night club, which was also an arcade. Talk about sensory overload—there were flashing lights, crowds, and noise everywhere! Halfway through the night, I ended up meeting a fellow introvert who wasn't sure if he wanted to be there either. We spent the night talking, just the two of us. Later, from a safe distance, we made jokes and sarcastic comments as we watched the crowd writhe on the dance floor. Needless to say, it unexpectedly ended up being a fun, memorable night.

There have been other times when something I thought would be fun didn't turn out that way. There's just no guarantee how a social event will go. The important thing is to accept that no perfect decision exists. There will be trade-offs no matter what you decide (whether you're an introvert or an extrovert!). Often you have to just make your decision and deal with whatever happens. And if you end up wanting to go home thirty minutes after you arrive, give yourself permission to do just that.

How to Prevent an Introvert Hangover

Sometimes you really, *really* do want to go to something, even though you're certain you'll get slapped with an introvert hangover. Jax is an introvert who's into cosplay. She faces this conundrum every year when she attends Dragon Con in Atlanta, which is a five-day sci-fi convention that boasts more than seventy thousand people in attendance. "The crowds are unbelievable," Jax tells me. "The partying and panels and contests are non-stop. It can be an emotional meat grinder for even an extrovert."

Thankfully, Jax and her friends have discovered some strategies that allow them to enjoy the conference and avoid introvert hangovers. For starters, they make sure their group has an equal mix of introverts and extroverts. That way, the extroverts always have other extroverts to talk to, and the introverts can find support among their fellow introverts if they need to sidestep the crowd and not talk for a bit. They book several hotel rooms so everyone has a safe, quiet place to retreat to, and they come prepared—they keep Crock-Pots and coolers in their rooms so anyone who needs to escape can relax and make a snack. This also helps them avoid lengthy food lines, which can be torture for a hungry introvert. Most important, when the convention is over, Jax schedules plenty of alone time to recover.

Every introvert has their own tricks for dealing with over-stimulation. Here are some more ideas from fellow introverts to help you avoid an introvert hangover, no matter where you are:

- "I always make sure I'm in my own vehicle. I leave once I've had enough."

  —Brandon

- "I always have an escape plan—as in, I will figure out ahead of time what my legitimate excuse is for leaving early. If needed, I will deploy it."

  —Kayla

- "What helps me with events is doing as much advance preparation as possible. If I haven't been to the event site before, I'll google the directions. I'll iron my outfit the evening before, and I'll give myself plenty of time to get there. Once I decide to attend an event, I'll decide at that point how long I'll stay. I also make sure to get alone time before and after the event."

  —Frances

- "I check my phone. It's my companion when I feel like I'm out of place, and it's the best weapon to ignore people around."

  —Angge

- "I take mini breaks to people watch. I'm fine being around people if I'm not having to socialize. So if I can find a place to sit and have a drink and just watch people for a little while, it lets me recharge."

  —Shannon

- "I take five minute breaks about every twenty minutes. I go where it is completely silent and just soak in the silence."

  —Noah

- "I set my phone alarm to sound after one hour of company to remind me to slip away and check in with myself. Preventatively, I take one whole day per week off from the world. I stay at home and avoid overstimulation. It is a sacred day of rest."

  —Sunny

- "I focus on finding one person who will talk to me one-on-one."

  —Marija

In Closing

Shawna, who first wrote about the introvert hangover, went on to attend more family gatherings with her now-husband's gregarious, if slightly overwhelming, family. "Obviously, I knew that was part of the deal by the time I married him," she writes. But things are getting easier. She now listens to her body's signals and makes her introvert needs clear. "I make my own clear demands for personal time and space," she writes. "Because as introverts, if we want to avoid a hangover, moderation is key."

Chapter 5

INTROVERTS AREN'T UNSOCIABLE—WE SOCIALIZE DIFFERENTLY

Introverts don't hate socializing; it's that we do it differently than extroverts. For example, although I avoid big parties like the plague, one of my favorite things is to get dinner with my best friend, a fellow introvert. We talk about everything that's on our minds. Something incredible happens after these conversations; even though I've been socializing for hours, I leave the restaurant feeling energized, not drained. That's because these conversations are "inner world" to "inner world." My friend and I share reflections, insights, and ideas—the secrets of our mental landscape. The focus is on the internal. Extroverts discuss ideas, too, but the ideas are usually less important than the interaction itself, and they emerge as the conversation takes place. For them, the focus is more external.

In this chapter, we'll explore how introverts socialize differently from extroverts. And if your life is missing that soul-nourishing "inner world" talk, read on. Later in this chapter,

I'll give you ideas for starting meaningful conversations and making friends who actually get you.

Breadth vs. Depth

When it comes to friendships, extroverts want the variety of the buffet, whereas introverts want the quality of the chef's special. In other words, the general rule is this: extroverts seek breadth while introverts crave depth. For example, I know two young stand-up comedians with very different temperaments—Misha the extrovert and Austin the introvert. After a show, they both hang out in the lobby to talk with friends and fans, but they take very different approaches. Misha, full of energy, works the room. He bounces from one person to the next, rarely talking with anyone for more than a few minutes. And because of this, he's the most socially connected person I know. (He invited over three hundred people to his birthday party—he had to rent a theater to hold them all!) Austin, on the other hand, stays mostly in the same location, talking with the few people he's developed a meaningful relationship with. Of course, there are times when these two break their normal patterns of behavior, and Austin can be found going from group to group while Misha talks at length with just one person. But in general, it's breadth vs. depth.

It's not that Austin is a misanthrope. He's a caring, warm person who volunteers as an English instructor. But if he had to switch places with Misha—schmoozing with all those fans—he'd probably find himself succumbing to an introvert hangover.

Like Austin, introverts tend to keep their social circles small because they want to dive deep. Daniel Pinkney, writing on his blog *MisterP.ink*, calls this "all-or-nothing syndrome." He writes, "In order to develop that degree of closeness, intimacy, and freedom, a lot of time/energy needs to be expended. And therein lies the problem. If I have a friend or partner, I want to be able to give them my all, so anyone outside that small circle usually gets relegated to 'acquaintances.' If I can't give my best to any one person, I'd rather not give at all."

Despite what society might tell you, it's perfectly okay to have just a few close friends. There's nothing wrong with saving the bulk of your energy for the people you truly "click" with. As introverts, we only have so much "people" energy to give. When we invest in a relationship, we want it to be exceptional.

It's about Balance

Introverts keep their social circles small, and that's okay. Just make sure your social circle isn't *zero*. Interestingly, research shows that everyone—both extroverts *and* introverts—can feel happier after socializing. Researcher William Fleeson and his colleagues tracked a group of people every three hours for two weeks, recording what they did and how they felt during each chunk of time. They found that those who'd acted "talk-ative" and "assertive" were more likely to report feeling positive emotions such as enthusiasm and excitement *in the moment.* It didn't matter whether the subject identified as an introvert or an extrovert; everyone reported a "happiness bump" after acting outgoing.

Does this mean that introverts should rent theaters and throw birthday parties to the tune of three hundred people? Not exactly. Introverts really do get worn out by socializing, and the quality of our interactions matter. But it does mean we need *some* socializing. It's all about balance. We can't party all weekend, but we also shouldn't shut ourselves away in our homes for years à la the poet Emily Dickinson. Find what works for you—dinner with your best friend, writing a thoughtful email to your sister to catch her up on your week, or messaging with online friends. The important thing is to be social on your own terms. You may find that if you initiate the interaction, you'll have more control over it—and ultimately this can help prevent social brain-drain.

Rules for Being Friends with an Introvert

Introverts need friends, too, but let's face it, navigating a friendship can be tricky. You have expectations for how the relationship should go, and so do they—and those expectations don't always match up. That's when feelings turn sour. So in the interest of introverts everywhere and the people who become friends with them, I'm going to lay down some ground rules.

Suggested use: mention these points casually to your friends and talk about which rules resonate with you and which ones don't. Highly discouraged: hanging this section of the book where your friends will see it and handing out citations to rule-breakers like a traffic cop.

Here are fourteen rules for being friends with an introvert:

1. **If you want to get to know us better, hang out with us one-on-one.** Have you ever wanted to make an introvert disappear? Put them in a large group. They'll quietly fade into the background, and pretty soon it's like they're not even there. But when you get introverts alone, it's a different story. Introverts thrive in more intimate settings because when we're talking to just one person, it drastically reduces our stimulation level; we only have to pay attention to the words, body language, and tone of voice of one person. Plus, during a one-on-one, it's easier to talk about more meaningful things. Group talk tends to revolve around "safe" topics like the news, jokes, and only the parts of your spring break trip to Cancun that are clean enough to tell your grandma. Introverts want to share ideas and talk authentically about things that matter.

2. **Likewise, if you say it's just going to be the two of us, don't invite other people.** It's a little hurtful if we feel like we're just another warm body in your extrovert entourage. We want to mean something to you, because if we're friends, you mean a lot to us. Plus, we were probably looking forward to talking to just you, and we didn't mentally prepare ourselves to interact with people whom we may not be comfortable with. Before you invite other people, check with us. We might be totally up for it (if we've got the energy) or we might not. Either way, we'll feel like you've respected our preferences.

3. **We'd rather have a tiny moment of real connection than hours of polite chitchat.** How are you *really*? What's *really* on your mind? Don't just tell us that you had a good weekend. Tell us it was good because you finally sorted out your complicated feelings about your ex. Or that you're having an existential crisis over the fact that you're getting older and that you haven't accomplished the things you thought you would have accomplished by now. We'd rather know what's going on inside you—what's *really* going on—than just see the polished facade that you display to everyone else. How are your ideas, thoughts, and feelings evolving?

4. **Sometimes we need encouragement to open up about ourselves.** As much as introverts enjoy meaningful, authentic conversation, we can struggle to get there. In fact, we tend to keep our thoughts, opinions, and feelings to ourselves, especially around people we don't know well. For example, there have been many times when something was bothering me, and I wanted to talk to someone about it. But because I worried I was inconveniencing the people around me—or I just didn't know what to say to steer the conversation my way—I didn't bring it up. I've gotten better at advocating for myself as I've gotten older, but sometimes it's still hard. If you notice that your new introvert friend looks particularly distracted, maybe there's something that's weighing heavily on their mind that they don't know how to talk about. Try asking them good-natured, non-prying questions. "You don't quite seem like yourself today. Is there something on your mind that you'd want to

talk about?" Of course, if they say they don't want to talk about it, don't push too hard. But showing a little interest in us, and directly inviting us to talk, can go a long way.

5. **We may have a hard time confronting you about something.** In the same way that we may struggle to open up, we may also shy away from conflict. This isn't true of all introverts. I know introverts who are just as blunt and confrontational as some extroverts. But in general, introverts don't like to rock the boat. Remember the study that said introverts saw an angry person's gaze as a threat? It's like that. Angry, harsh words can be overstimulating. And we're likely to brood on hurtful comments, making the matter worse. But if a friend crosses a boundary, they probably won't hear about it right away. We likely won't erupt on the spot (unless it's *really* bad). Rather we'll go home, think about what was said or done, and bring it up a day or two later (or send you an email—it's easier to write our thoughts than speak them).

6. **We may get lost in our own little world.** The introvert's inner world is vivid and alive. It's as real as the world around us that we can see, smell, touch, taste, and feel. This means we're prone to daydreaming and getting lost in our thoughts. While we're hanging out, if we drift off for a moment, don't say things like "Hey, where did you go?" or "Helloooooo come back to earth!" This will probably make us feel self-conscious. Don't worry, we're just taking a short trip to the realm of our thoughts, and we'll be back with you in a few moments.

7. **Our silence means we're processing.** Likewise, if we're having a conversation with you and we're quiet for a moment, we're probably thinking about what you said. Give us a beat to collect our thoughts (we like to think before we speak), and then we'll lay some introvert wisdom on you.

8. **We like talking, too.** I have an extroverted friend who will go on and on about her life if given the chance. Suddenly, twenty minutes have gone by and I've barely said anything. I like to listen and be supportive of her, but even I have my limits, as all introverts do. Please remember that although introverts are good listeners, we still like to talk, too. Unfortunately, many people interpret our silence (and our lack of interrupting) as an invitation to keep talking. Make sure your quiet friend gets their turn, too.

9. **We may not call or text you as much as your extroverted friends.** That doesn't mean we're not thinking about you. On the contrary, you probably float through our busy mind quite a bit when we're apart. But we know we'll soon see each other again, and we'd rather catch up in a way that's meaningful—in person, over coffee, one-on-one.

10. **Give us time to mentally prepare to hang out.** Spontaneity can be fun, and it has its place. But as a general rule, don't text us and ask us to be ready to hang out in ten minutes. We need time to mentally prepare for socializing—even if it's with a close friend. Every introvert is different, but I prefer to be asked to socialize at least a day in advance.

11. **As much as we love you, please don't show up at our house without asking.** Our home is our sacred space where we can (hopefully) quietly recharge. This goes back to the whole "we need to be mentally prepared to see people" thing.

12. **If we don't answer your text, email, or Facebook message right away, don't think we're ignoring you.** We might want to think for a while about how we'll respond. I often read messages and don't answer right away because I want to think of the best way to answer. Or we may be in introvert recharge mode—no people, no messaging, no phone. For our own mental sanity, sometimes we need to completely disconnect from people in every way.

13. **Please know that as much as we had fun hanging out with you yesterday, we probably don't want to hang out again today.** You may feel energized from hanging out the day before, but we feel tired—even if we enjoyed ourselves. Give us some time to be in introvert mode, and we promise, we'll want to see you again soon.

14. **If we say we want to stay home, we really do just want to stay home.** We're not trying to hide from you. We're not sending you the passive-aggressive message that we don't want to be friends anymore. We likely just need some downtime to recharge.

If You Want More Friends

What if you're staying home every weekend not because you need to recharge, but because you don't have anyone to hang out with? Shawna Courter (yes, ironically, the same person who wrote about the introvert hangover) understands this problem. "One of my biggest regrets about the past decade of my life is that I didn't make more of an effort to make friends of my own," she writes in an *Introvert, Dear* article. "I got caught up in work, in my marriage, in taking care of my family." It wasn't until she was packing to move away from her home in Los Angeles that she realized that she hadn't gotten to know many people in the five plus years she'd lived there. "Why didn't I go out and do more things, meet more people? Honestly, it was because I was afraid," she writes. "I was plagued by *what ifs*. What if I showed up at an event and no one talked to me? What if I said or did something embarrassing? What if, what if, what if . . . ? I allowed those fears to stop me."

As Shawna drove across the country to her new home, she realized she didn't want to let fear control her anymore. She challenged herself to step out of her introvert comfort zone and meet more people. She's been in her new city for over two years now, and she feels like she's finally created the kind of life she wants to live.

Finding "your people" is hard. As an adult, where do you go to meet new people? And how do you start a conversation with someone you barely know? Hanging out with people you don't know well can be draining. Also, you don't want to be friends with just anyone—that means the chatty extrovert who parties every weekend probably won't become your BFF. You're looking for a friend who understands you—someone you truly "click" with.

So, what's an introvert to do? Here are nine ideas to help you make friends with people who truly "get" you:

1. **Think about the people you already know.** You don't have to head to the nearest party or networking event to make new friends. Chances are there are already people in your life whom you'd like to get to know better. Ask yourself, which of your acquaintances seem interesting? Make it a point to talk to these people more.

2. **It's okay to make the first move.** Many introverts (myself included) are guilty of waiting for other people to come to them. We worry about rejection. "What if I ask her to get coffee after class and she says no?" Or worse, "What if he gets to know me better and he doesn't like who I am?" As Shawna experienced, the process of making new friends can fill a person with self-doubt. And if you're an introvert who has experienced significant rejection (as many of us have), you may feel so discouraged you don't even want to try anymore.

In college, I learned a hard lesson about being passive about making friends. When I moved away from home and left my childhood friends behind, I quickly found myself alone and lonely. I looked around and wondered how everyone had become friends with each other so quickly. Eventually, I realized I wasn't making an effort to get to know anyone. I was skipping social mixers and dorm events that were designed for freshmen mingling. I saw classes as an opportunity, to, well, *learn* something, when they could have been an opportunity to both learn *and* meet new people. I had wrongly assumed that making friends would just *happen*, without any action on my part. I'm not saying you have to turn yourself into an extrovert—but you can give yourself permission to "go first."

3. **Peel off the mask.** Some introverts keep their thoughts and preferences hidden because they worry about others judging them. They don't reveal who they really are, fearing what others may think. But this can lead to having hollow relationships—and becoming friends with people who don't really "get" you. Instead, when you meet someone you want to connect with, be brave and show them who you really are. Say what you really think and feel, even if you worry they'll disagree or won't be able to relate. You can do this bit by bit—it doesn't have to be a flood. And you can do it tactfully. When you peel off the mask, you make yourself vulnerable, and this is how true connection is created.

4. **Ask questions.** Introverts have a superpower: listening. Ask the other person questions about themselves. What's new in their life? If they could have any career they want, what would it be? Use your powerful listening skills to learn more about them. Plus, when you get them talking, it takes the spotlight off you.

5. **Notice how you feel.** Do you feel energized after hanging out with your new friend? Or are you so exhausted that you want to hide in your bedroom for days? As an introvert,

it's normal to feel tired after spending time with someone new (after all, peeling off the mask takes precious energy). But overall, your friend should make you feel good, not drained. It's okay to listen to your feelings—use them to guide your interactions with your new friend.

6. **Watch out for potentially toxic relationships.** It's not uncommon for introverts to get stuck in one-sided or toxic relationships. During an interview with me, Adam S. McHugh, author of *Introverts in the Church,* says, "We give people space to express themselves, which is our gift and our curse. People feel safe around us, and share openly with us, because they know we won't interrupt them or compete for attention. We are often content letting other people shape how conversations go." In other words, when you're the calm one who listens sympathetically, you can end up on the losing end of a relationship with a toxic person. That's because emotionally needy people usually lack self-awareness—they may not even realize that they're dominating the relationship. They may often try to turn the conversation back to them and their problems, and their pain can become a controlling factor in the friendship.

That's why it's important to set boundaries. If you don't, you may feel like you're losing yourself in unhealthy relationships. "No matter what your temperament, the key to avoiding toxic relationships is a strong sense of self," Adam says. "If you lack that, you will probably find yourself in one-sided relationships with unhealthy people." One of the most helpful

THE SECRET LIVES OF INTROVERTS

changes he has made is making sure that he's not the only one initiating in a relationship. By "initiation," he means not only whether people text or invite him to coffee, but also whether people ask questions about his life and show genuine interest in his responses. "Those are the people worth investing in," he tells me.

7. **Remember that the awkwardness will go away with time.** Introverts tend to keep their best stuff inside—quirky, fun personalities—and only let their true selves out once they feel comfortable around someone. If being with your new friend is somewhat awkward at first, don't beat yourself up. The more you hang out with them, the more comfortable you'll feel. Keep at it.

8. **Plan a regularly scheduled meet-up.** Ask your new friend (and maybe a few others) to hang out once a week. Have brunch every Saturday morning or get a drink after work every Thursday. Having a standing "friend date" means you don't have to exert as much energy to plan something—the details are already taken care of. Plus, routine tends to make us introverts feel more comfortable because then we know what to expect.

9. **Go slowly.** Genuine friendship takes time to develop. If you bow to the pressure to start collecting groupies, you'll likely end up with shallow, unsatisfying relationships that fall apart because there was never a true connection. Allow relationships to develop naturally.

How to Ditch Small Talk

As an introvert who craves meaningful interaction, this will probably come as no surprise to you: psychologist Matthias Mehl and his team discovered a link between happiness and substantive conversation. His study, published in the journal *Psychological Science*, involved college students who wore an electronically activated recorder with a microphone on their shirt collar that captured thirty-second snippets of conversation every twelve and a half minutes for four days. Effectively, this created a conversational "diary" of their day. Then, researchers went through the conversations and categorized them as either small talk (talk about the weather, a recent TV show, etc.) or more substantive conversation (talk about philosophy, current affairs, etc.). Researchers were careful not to automatically label certain topics a certain way; for example, if the speakers analyzed a TV show's characters and their motivations, this conversation was considered substantive. They also found that some conversations didn't fit neatly into either category; these were discussions that focused on practical matters, like who would take out the trash or what the homework assignment was. Ultimately, the researchers found that about one-third of the college students' conversations were considered substantive, while one-fifth consisted of small talk. The researchers also studied how happy the participants were, drawing data from life satisfaction reports the college students completed themselves, as well as feedback from people in the students' lives.

The results: Mehl and his team found that the happiest person in the study had twice as many substantive conversations, and only one-third of the amount of small talk, as the unhappiest person. Almost every other conversation the happiest person had—about 46 percent of the day's conversations—were substantive. For the unhappiest person, only 22 percent of this person's conversations were substantive. Similarly, small talk made up only 10 percent of the happiest person's conversations, while it made up almost three times as much (about 29 percent) of the unhappiest person's discussions.

Further research is still needed, because it's not clear whether people *make* themselves happier by having substantive conversations or whether people who are already happy choose to engage in meaningful talk. However, one thing is evident: happiness and meaningful interactions go hand-in-hand. Mehl, in an interview with the *New York Times,* discusses the reasons why he thinks substantive conversations are linked to happiness. For one, humans are driven to create meaning in their lives, and substantive conversations help us do that, he says. Also, human beings—both introvert and extrovert—are social animals who have a real need to connect with others. Substantive conversation connects, whereas small talk doesn't.

Want to have more substantive conversations? Here are five ideas to help you ditch the small talk.

1. **Get the other person to tell a story.** Small talk can be boring because we often ask questions that can be answered in just one or two words. For example, "How are you?" ("Fine") or "How was your day?" ("Pretty good.") To ditch the small talk, try asking more open-ended questions like, "What was the most interesting thing that happened at

work today?" Questions like these invite the other person to tell a story. Here are some more ideas:

Instead of . . .

"How are you?"
"How was your weekend?"
"Where did you grow up?"
"What do you do for a living?"

Try . . .

"What's your story?"
"What was your favorite part of your weekend?"
"Tell me something interesting about where you grew up."
"What drew you to your line of work?"

2. **Be curious.** As an introvert, you're probably naturally curious. You wonder how the world works or what makes a person tick. When talking with others, channel your instinctive curiosity. Put yourself in the mind-set of being curious to learn more about the other person. You'll probably find that you listen more intently, your body language will show that you're engaged, and you'll more easily think of questions that move the conversation forward. Plus, being curious about others is a highly attractive quality, and it creates immediate interest and intimacy.

3. **Ask why instead of what.** This is a twist on asking open-ended questions. Instead of asking about the facts ("what" questions), ask people *why* they made certain decisions.

For example, after you've asked, "What college did you go to?" follow up with, "Why did you choose that college?"

4. **Share details about yourself and see what sticks.** This can be hard for introverts, because we tend to dislike talking about ourselves. It puts the spotlight on us, and we may feel exposed. As a result, we get stuck in cycles of mind-numbing small talk in which we don't reveal anything about ourselves, and in turn, we don't learn anything meaningful about the other person. This prevents the relationship from growing in a satisfying way.

To avoid this, share a few details about yourself and see what sticks. If you work in an office or go to school, you probably get asked "How are you?" several times a day. Instead of giving the typical response ("I'm fine, how are you?"), expand on your answer and give a few details about your day. You might say something like, "Good, I got up early this morning to get coffee from my favorite coffee shop." Then, notice how the other person reacts. Do they keep the conversation going by asking a follow-up question ("Nice! What's your favorite coffee shop?") or do they give a disinterested nod? If the other person doesn't seem interested, try revealing another detail about yourself until you hit on a topic that gets the two of you talking. "I had a really hard time with last night's assignment. I couldn't figure out what the professor wanted. Did you understand what we're supposed to do?"

5. **Dare to be honest.** We often sacrifice expressing our true thoughts and feelings for the sake of politeness. But there's something very authentic, and surprisingly charming,

about being completely honest. In *The Irresistible Introvert*, Michaela Chung writes that you can quickly take conversations to a deeper level by saying things like:

- "To be honest, I don't go to parties very much. I feel pretty overwhelmed being here."
- "I'm not a big talker, but I like listening."
- "I don't like camping. Like, at all."
- "I'm really proud of that."
- "This feels awkward."
- "That hurt my feelings."
- "No. I don't want to go. I'd rather stay home and have some me time."

Be careful to not take this to the extreme. You risk alienating your conversation partner if you overshare or insult. However, if done right, even one authentic disclosure can quickly build intimacy, because honesty draws people in.

When Friends Drift Apart

It can be hard to make meaningful connections. It can be even harder when you lose a close friend. That's what happened to Maleri Sevier, who became friends with someone unexpected. A fellow classmate in graduate school, her new friend was one of those people whom everyone liked; in Maleri's own words, she was "a force in the world." Maleri, on the other hand, is a quiet introvert. To her surprise, they spent hours together studying, sharing stories, and enjoying deep conversation. Maleri opened up to her in ways she had never expected.

After graduation, the two moved to different cities, and that's when they drifted apart. During their last conversation, Maleri accused her friend of treating her as though she were not a priority. She admits that she was harsh with her words, but she was desperate to hold onto a relationship that meant so much to her. The two women have not spoken since that argument, and she worries that the friendship is beyond repair.

The loss was extremely painful for Maleri, because it's not often that she finds someone who truly "gets" her. "In those rare instances when a real friendship develops, and I feel truly understood by the other person, it is nearly impossible to let go of them," Maleri writes in an *Introvert, Dear* article. "Finding someone who is willing to indulge my interests (as obscure as they sometimes are) as freely as I am willing to indulge theirs, is a gift. It is rare to feel so truly accepted."

Have you ever lost a good friend? You may find yourself ruminating on what happened, feeling like you can't get your thoughts to change tracks and move on. Maleri writes that she spent hours going over the different scenarios for how things could have gone differently with her friend—but this was not productive because she couldn't change the past, and brooding drained her energy. Maleri found it helpful to write about her feelings and to talk about the situation with another close friend. Getting her thoughts out of her head helped her to process them better and to break free of the rumination cycle.

If you have recently lost a friendship, you may want to take this time to appreciate your other relationships. While you may not have as deep of a relationship with your other friends, you likely have a group of people around you who love you. "Those friends who were there for me during my friendship grieving process have endeared themselves to me in ways they will never know," Maleri writes. "The sense of trust their actions have engendered have allowed me to be more open with them and to be more willing to trust them with the deeper parts of my being."

To prevent a devastating loss from happening again, ask yourself if you're seeking relationships with reciprocity. Relationships require reciprocity in order for both parties to be fulfilled. If a relationship becomes too one-sided, you may begin to resent one another. Of course, we all go through waves of needing more at certain times in our lives—and these waves are a normal part of life—but if your relationship is constantly out of balance, you may not be as good friends as you think. If you're always the one initiating contact—setting up times to meet, sending the first text, etc.—the relationship may be one-sided. Likewise, both parties need to "get something" out of the relationship. This means one person is not doing all the talking, asking for all the favors, or always leaning on the other for emotional support. The amount of "give and take" should be roughly equal.

Finally, recognize that it's normal to be close to certain friends for a time, even if you drift away later. Often, friendship is born when we have things in common—we attend the same school, work in the same office, or live in the same neighborhood. When we lose our common ground (for example, when you get a different job and no longer see your coworker-turned-friend every day), the friendship may change. You may not have done anything wrong.

Of course, just because your life or your friend's life is changing doesn't mean you have to lose the relationship—but you may have to put in extra effort to maintain it. The introverted best friend I mentioned at the beginning of this chapter was my college roommate. Today, our lives are very different from the way they were in college, and although we live an hour's drive away from each other, we meet once a week, in between our two cities, for dinner.

In Closing

Introverts may balk when they get invited to parties. They may wish their friends would stop texting for a while and leave them alone. It's true that certain types of socializing drain us, but introverts need friends, too. Because of our limited "people" energy, we don't let just anyone into our lives. But we treasure the relationships we do have. If you're in our inner circle, know that you're very special to us.

Chapter 6

PLEASE JUST LEAVE ME ALONE

Rachel Ginder (yes, the same Rachel who fled Oktoberfest) decided she would finally build the social life of her dreams. She created an account on the social networking site Meetup. com, joined some groups, and for several months committed to being as social as possible. "I went to anything I could find on Fridays or Saturdays," she writes in an *Introvert, Dear* article. "I even went to the occasional outing on a weeknight, and if nothing else was going on, I forced myself to go out to a movie by myself with the continued hope that I might make myself approachable to friendly strangers."

There was one particular Meetup group she joined that consisted of women in their twenties and thirties. It wasn't uncommon for them to get together several nights a week. "They thought nothing of hosting a game night on a Thursday evening that stretched well past 11 p.m., and then organizing a brunch two days later and/or a possible shopping trip that promised to last well into the evening," she writes.

In theory, this was exactly what Rachel had been looking for—she gained lots of friends and was getting out of the house often. In reality, it turned out to be her worst nightmare. She quickly found herself exhausted. "After coming home in the evening, I typically need a couple of hours to unwind before I can go to sleep," she writes. "Although being around people often leaves me physically tired, my brain will not shut off unless I've had enough time to mentally process all that's just happened. Unfortunately, staying up after midnight 'mentally processing' isn't a very good excuse for coming into work late on a Wednesday. No matter how well-organized or scheduled these group parties were, they left me feeling drained." Plus, in a group of fifteen or more people, it was impossible to get quality one-on-one time to engage in meaningful conversation. "Missing that conversation was keeping me from gaining any emotional fulfillment from the evening," she explains.

Rachel lasted with this "dream" group of friends for about two weeks. One night, as the last of the wine was being drunk, someone asked Rachel if she was going to the next happy hour. She said no, offering a vague excuse about having a lot of work. Secretly she was planning to stay home, watch Netflix, and recharge. Rachel then deflected by asking the woman if she was planning to go. She replied, "Yes, I don't have anything else to do." This struck Rachel as odd. "And there was the problem. Because I had discovered that whenever I was socializing, I always felt like I had something else I could be doing." In her attempts to live the dream life of an extrovert, she found herself neglecting the fulfilling things she really enjoyed. "My home was full of overdue library books, unfinished writing projects, and the ingredients for at least a half dozen Pinterest recipes I didn't have the time to make. I was even beginning to miss the boring things, like watching the news while folding laundry."

In Rachel's attempt to be more social, she found herself living a more unbalanced and unhappy existence than ever before. She wasn't getting enough alone time to recharge, and because of this, she was suffering. She realized that she needed to stop prioritizing meaningless social events that she was just using to keep busy—she already had a half dozen hobbies and interests that kept her busy every night of the week. "A person who is truly busy doesn't have time to go out for dinner every night and bar crawl every weekend, because that person is already going to the gym, working on a craft project, or making themselves dinner," she writes. "It's perfectly okay to turn down social events for any of those reasons. It's healthy even. It means you are living a balanced life."

These days, she usually spends her Friday nights going grocery shopping. Then she comes home, makes dinner, and binge-watches *Friends* while she folds laundry. "Sometimes I do this because I want to get the chores out of the way before I spend Saturday with some of the new people I've met or curl up at the local coffee shop with only a book for company," she writes. "No matter which one it is, I consider myself to be having a pretty busy weekend."

It's no secret that solitude is the introvert's fuel for life. In this chapter, we'll explore the introvert's love of solitude—including why downtime makes your life better and how to get more of it.

Introverts' Favorite Things to Do Alone

Whether it's reading a book, playing video games, or just quietly daydreaming, introverts gain energy from solitude. I asked introverts what activities they like to do when they're alone. Here's what they told me:

> "Read, watch movies, surf the Internet, or just relax."
>
> —Sophia

> "Painting, playing with my cats, reading, sometimes just laying down and thinking for hours. Also I like to organize if I have something messy around the house."
>
> —Kadisa

> "I usually watch TED Talks. It's nice hearing opinions from others on how they live their lives, react to things, and solve their problems."
>
> —Grant

> "I always dive into the world of the Internet. I can see how people are doing, send a few emails, catch up on the news, and whatever else. This way I can go at my own pace, and I don't have to make eye contact, deal with annoying small talk, or really interact with anyone unless I choose to."
>
> —Kayla

"Zone out, drink tea, and listen to good music."
—Emily

"Play games on the computer or watch *Star Trek*. Basically any escapist behavior. I recharge ten times faster if I'm engaged in something fantastical."
—Steve

"Gardening, swimming alone, meditating in the corner, making a scrapbook in a locked room."
—Orola

"Solitude is prime writing time, when there's no danger of the real world unceremoniously yanking me out of my imaginary world every five minutes."
—Eric

"If I'm alone, you can guarantee I'm binge-watching one of my favorite TV shows."
—Courtney

"I love to read, go on Facebook, watch movies, spend time with my cats, and think about life."
—Thomas

Solitude Really Does Make Your Life Better

It's also no secret that our society values *doing* over *being*. If you're not actually *producing* anything, aren't you just wasting time? It's not like staring out the window, deep in thought, checks anything off your to-do list. Other people don't help, either. They play into the idea that downtime is unproductive. "You haven't done *anything* all afternoon?" your spouse may ask. Or your friend may say, "You're just going to stay home tonight and do *nothing*?" But for introverts, "nothing" really is something.

The truth is downtime isn't a waste of time. Solitude can actually make your life better. For one, it can help you solve problems. See if this sounds familiar: You have a big decision to make, say, whether you should quit the job that's making you crazy and take a new gig that promises more sanity but less pay. You can't seem to make up your mind, so you talk to friend after friend. Each time someone makes a convincing argument, you change your verdict. Ultimately, you end up more confused than when you started. Eventually you get some time to yourself. After "sitting" with the problem alone, thinking over all the advice you've been given, you finally know what to do.

That's because the unconscious mind needs time alone to process and unravel problems, according to psychologist Ester Buchholz, who writes about solitude in a *Psychology Today* blog post. Getting away from other people and distractions can clear your mind and help you focus better. For this reason, when Buchholz's patients are faced with a problem, she gives them advice that seems counterintuitive: spend time alone and don't focus on the issue head-on. Once alone, their mind often solves their problem for them.

Solitude can also help improve your relationships. Like Buchholz's advice to her patients, this may seem counterintuitive, since being alone means you can't spend time with other people. But when you get time away from the people in your life, you may find that you appreciate them more the next time you see them. It's like the old saying: absence makes the heart grow fonder. Plus, when your introvert battery is recharged, you can "show up" better for everyone.

Also, when you are alone, your brain can finally stop multitasking. Research from Harvard professor Daniel Gilbert and graduate student Bethany Burum suggests that simply being around another person sucks up a certain amount of the brain's attention, making some tasks harder. In the study, which Leon Neyfakh wrote about in a *Boston Globe* article called "The Power of Lonely," the researchers had two people sit in a room back to back, each facing a computer screen that the other person could not see. In some instances, they were told they'd be doing different tasks (one person would be identifying images while the other person would identify sounds). In other instances, they were told they'd both be identifying images. The computer showed pictures of everyday objects, like a clock, log, or guitar. A few days later, when the participants returned, they were asked to name the objects they were shown. Burum found that the participants who had been told that the person behind them was doing a different task did a better job of recalling the images than the participants who believed that the other person was doing the same task. In other words, they formed stronger memories when they thought they were the only ones doing the exercise. Burum believes this happened because sharing an experience with someone is inherently distracting. We have to spend energy thinking about what the other person is going through and how they're reacting to it. The results are preliminary, but they suggest that other people actually steal your brainpower.

It may come as no surprise, then, that being alone may help you think more deeply; it's nearly impossible to have nuanced, rich thoughts when you're engaging with others. As the deep-thinking poet Rumi once noted, "A little while alone in your room will prove more valuable than anything else that could ever be given you." And, when it comes to learning and studying, being alone can help. If you're a student with a big test coming up, consider studying alone. According to research by sociology professors Richard Arum and Josipa Roksa, students who study by themselves are more likely to succeed and to retain knowledge than those who study in groups. That's because students who spend time in solitary reflection likely have improved concentration.

You don't necessarily need other people around to have a good time. A study conducted by professors Rebecca Ratner and Rebecca Hamilton found that people can have an equally good time partaking in fun activities on their own as they would if they were with others. They asked people on an American college campus—people who were alone or in pairs—how interested they'd be in visiting a nearby art exhibition. Often, the people who were alone weren't enthusiastic about going, but the researchers encouraged them to go anyway. After visiting the exhibition, they surveyed both groups—the singletons and the people in pairs—and found that everyone enjoyed themselves. So, if your favorite band is in town but you can't get anyone to go with you to the concert, consider going anyway. The not-so-fun part comes in when you worry about how others will perceive your aloneness. Do they think you're a loser who has no one to hang out with? If you can get over worrying about what others think of you, doing things alone can be a blast. And, Burum's study shows us that those experiences may become some of your most vivid memories.

When you're alone, you get to have things your way. Being in the company of others means you will always have to compromise on some level. They want Italian for dinner but you want Chinese? You want to shop but they want to hike? You can't always get what you want, and only one of you will get their way. However, when you're alone, you can eat sweet and sour chicken in bed while shopping online—if you want.

Most important, if you're an introvert, solitude invigorates you. So there shouldn't be any shame in turning yourself into a blanket burrito and lounging at home. Your energy levels depend on it.

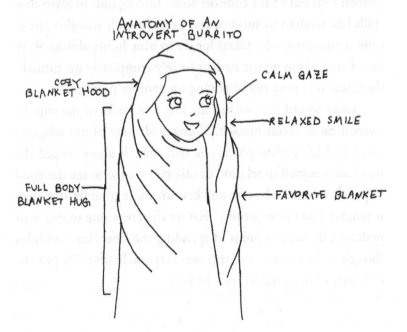

ANATOMY OF AN
INTROVERT BURRITO

COZY
BLANKET HOOD

CALM GAZE

RELAXED SMILE

FULL BODY
BLANKET HUG

FAVORITE BLANKET

Solitude Can Help You Discover Yourself

Another powerful benefit of solitude is that it can help you discover yourself. That's what solitude did for Andre Sólo (yes, the same Andre who made a plan to work on his social skills). When he was young, he dreamed of living a life of travel, but his ever-practical parents told him to forget about it—travel was just too expensive. Eventually he realized he didn't have to buy a plane ticket; he could travel across the continent by simply using his own strength. So, in his twenties, he quit his unfulfilling office job and started bicycling. He started at the headwaters of the Mississippi River and, to date, has gone all the way to the southernmost point of Mexico. And, being an introvert, he did it almost entirely alone. He says the trip pushed him out of his comfort zone, forcing him to learn new skills like wilderness survival and bike repair. It was also physically demanding—he biked for six to nine hours almost every day. Being alone meant he had to rely completely on himself; there was no safety net of relying on another person.

Andre found that within the first few weeks of the trip, he learned more about himself. "I changed some of my religious views and life philosophies," he tells me. "It also changed the way I view myself in relation to others. I started to see the good in people wherever I went, and became more friendly and open whenever I met new people." Rather than listening to music or podcasts, he made a point of spending the time alone with his thoughts. As a result, the trip was very meditative. "It put me in a state of deep reflection," he says.

Traveling alone did something else, too—it helped him clarify his life's purpose. Andre had been writing marketing copy for clients for quite some time; it was how he supported himself while he biked. Over the course of the trip, he realized he wanted to do more with his writing. "I realized I wanted to create great literature," he says. He has since gone on to write short fiction and has published the novella *Lúnasa Days*.

Going on a 4,700-mile bike trip isn't the only way to learn more about yourself. You could take a weekend retreat, go to a restaurant or movie alone, or do anything that you wouldn't normally do by yourself. You may find that you make very different choices when you're on your own. You may discover that rap music does not actually appeal to you or that you're more capable than the people around you make you feel. When you have a firm sense of self, it impacts all aspects of your life and changes how you relate to the world.

Faces, Flowers, and the P300 Response

The powerful benefits of solitude aren't exclusive to introverts; extroverts can reap the benefits, too. But while extroverts generally just tolerate being alone, introverts crave it. As we've already seen, one of the reasons introverts like being alone has to do with our less active dopamine reward system. When we spend time alone, we lower our stimulation level to one that is just right.

A study suggests another reason why introverts are less motivated to seek the company of others. Inna Fishman of the Salk Institute for Biological Studies and her colleagues recruited a group of twenty-eight participants of various ages, both introverts and extroverts. As they showed them pictures of both people and objects (like flowers), they recorded the electrical activity in their brains through an EEG and evaluated their brains' P300 activity. P300 activity happens when a person experiences a sudden change in their environment, and it gets its name from the fact that it lasts 300 milliseconds.

Interestingly, Fishman and her colleagues found that extroverts' and introverts' brains responded to the pictures differently. The higher subjects had scored on a test for extroversion, the greater their P300 response was to human faces. Introverts, on the other hand, had very similar P300 responses to both human faces and to objects. These results could mean that extroverts place more significance on people than introverts do—which may help explain why introverts are completely fine with hanging out at home in their pajamas on a Friday night, watching Netflix.

Introverts and Alone Time, by the Numbers

As I researched solitude, I started to wonder, how much alone time do introverts get on average? Are they getting enough? And if they aren't, what's stopping them? To find out, I created a survey and asked people who self-identified as introverts to respond (these were mostly readers of *Introvert, Dear*). I got 499 responses.

First I asked, "In an average week, how much restorative alone time do you get? This would be time spent by yourself, relaxing, doing enjoyable hobbies, etc." The results were:

Less than 1 hour: 2 percent
1–3 hours: 11 percent
4–6 hours: 18 percent
7–10 hours: 17 percent
10–14 hours: 17 percent
More than 14 hours: 35 percent

Turns out, many introverts (35 percent), get more than two hours a day of restorative alone time. However, some introverts (13 percent), get three or less hours a week, which translates to only minutes each day. Ouch.

Next I asked, "Overall, do you feel like you get enough restorative alone time?" The results were as follows:

No, I wish I got more alone time: 44 percent
Yes, the amount of alone time I get is about what I need: 46 percent
I get too much alone time: 10 percent

Interesting! About half of the respondents said they get the right amount of alone time, while almost another half wish they got more. Surprisingly, a few introverts feel they spend *too much* time alone (yes, you really can have "too much of a good thing.")

If introverts responded that they wished they got more alone time, I asked them one more question: "What prevents you from getting enough alone time?" They could choose as many options as they wanted. Here's how they answered:

My schedule is too busy for alone time: 60 percent
I feel guilty telling friends, family, or my significant other that I want to be alone: 49 percent
My obligations get in the way of alone time: 62 percent
I don't have a quiet space of my own to retreat to: 28 percent
I don't make enough of a conscious effort to spend time alone: 16 percent

They could also write in their own answers. Here's what some of them wrote:

"Living or hanging out with other people nearby draws me to them, even if I'm socially exhausted."
"As a family caregiver, I can't be away from the person I care for to have the solitude I need."
"My husband doesn't like it when I retreat to my quiet space."
"Family members come to my quiet space unannounced and uninvited."
"I have a roommate and don't feel completely alone unless she's out of the house. Even if I'm in a different room, I still don't feel completely alone."
"I need more [alone time] than is actually possible when you have a job."
"I'm constantly wasting the time I have worrying about things."

"I typically need more [alone time] than I think I need."

"Some friends will guilt me into doing things."

If you're an introvert who doesn't get enough alone time, you're not alone. In fact, what you experience is pretty common, so read on. We'll take a look at some common problems introverts face when it comes to alone time—and how you can start taking back your solitude.

When You Have Too Many Obligations

J. Lee Hazlett has always had a strong sense of commitment. In high school, she was on the student council and was an active member of several student organizations and the founder of another. When she wasn't busy with her various societies, she took evening courses at the local community college and worked twenty hours a week. In between all that, she had homework for numerous Advanced Placement classes. Her life was scheduled down to the quarter hour—a choice she made for herself.

"The main reason I said yes to such a laundry list of tasks was my sense of obligation," she writes in an *Introvert, Dear* article. "No Model UN meeting was going to result in peace in the Middle East, but discussing world politics was what good citizens were supposed to do. It would also look good on college applications, and it seemed that everyone who was anyone had gone to a top university. I promised myself that I would join their ranks, and thus compounded my already overburdened sense of obligation."

You can imagine how little time J. had for herself. She snatched at the few seconds of solitude she could find, reading between classes and volunteering for solitary tasks at work. Not even home was a refuge; instead it was another obligation where she had chores and family commitments. "I was miserable, tired, and desperately in need of some peace and quiet," she writes.

Nevertheless, she pressed on. "I had to," she writes. "I'd already agreed to all the things I was doing. When I wanted to drop something, I thought of my parents' disappointment or of how that one extra activity might be what got me into an Ivy League. I attended club meetings and work shifts with bronchitis and little sleep." Not even spraining her ankle was enough to sideline her. The crutches she should have used for weeks were tossed after six days so she could help prepare for Homecoming. "I don't remember who won that game or what my oh-so-essential tasks were, but every time my improperly healed foot twinges, I remember limping down the halls as fast as I could to get to my next commitment."

Saying No Is the First Step

J.'s overscheduling problem followed her to college and then to graduate school. She continued to fill her time with societies, extra classes, and a full-time job. She didn't want any of the balls she was juggling to drop. As a result, she remained stressed and burned out.

Eventually, J. realized that something had to change. She made a mental list of all the things in life that were important to her. Then she cut and slashed and deleted until there were only three things left: work, pursuing her dream of writing, and spending time with her husband. Now those three things are the only commitments she puts on her daily calendar. She's found that she has more time for herself, and she's happier than she could have ever dreamed possible.

It's still not easy to muster the self-discipline to say no. "When an opportunity to do more comes up, be it volunteering or attending a gathering at the home of a friend, my first impulse is to say yes," she writes. "My sense of obligation tries to commandeer my tongue. I still feel like I *should* fundraise and letter-campaign and go to my extroverted friends' fetes, even when I know I won't enjoy it. It still feels like my duty, and I still feel guilt when I finally manage to say no."

If she's learned anything from all this, it's that the guilt of saying no is much less painful and more short-lived than the guilt of backing out is. "Saying no is also the first step to clearing your overbooked calendar. Given time, everything that doesn't really matter to you will fall away. If you keep filling that empty space with new commitments, though, you'll never be free to focus on your true cares, your true calling, or yourself. And when it comes down to it, taking care of yourself is the most important obligation you'll ever have."

The Misplaced Guilt of Saying No

If you're anything like me, you feel guilty when you say no. But turning someone down isn't necessarily something you should feel guilty about. Guilt is an emotion we experience when we've done something wrong; if you harm someone, it's fitting to feel guilt. Saying no to the neighborhood chili cook-off isn't actually damaging someone. Your neighbors may have to re-envision the night (minus you), but you're not bringing them harm. Likewise, when you tell someone you can't do them a favor (such as babysit their kids), that's not a form of harm, either. They'll likely recalibrate and find help elsewhere.

We may feel guilty not only because we think we're hurting the other person, but also because we expect retaliation. We mistakenly think, *He's going to hate me*, or *She'll get mad*. Our minds automatically jump to the worst-case scenario. Instead, take a step back and look at all the other, much more likely possibilities your brain skipped over. The more likely scenario is the person will be momentarily disappointed, but will later understand—it won't be the end of the world. Just think about what you do when someone tells you no. You probably don't fly into a rage and cut that person out of your life. So why are you holding yourself to a different standard? You should expect others to react as you do. That is to say, sensibly.

Improve Your "No" Game

Steve Jobs once said, "Focus is about saying no." I'd argue that "no" is also a key to getting enough alone time. Here are six tips to improve your "no" game:

1. **Say it fast.** Don't leave people hanging for days or weeks and then tell them you won't be donning reindeer antlers

at the holiday office party or joining the committee. The sooner the better. When you say it fast, it gives the other party time to recalibrate—they can get someone else to bring eggnog or fill your role as treasurer. Plus, the sooner you give a firm answer, the sooner you can stop overthinking about it.

2. **Turn it into a compliment.** Soften the blow of "no" by prefacing it with something like, "Thank you so much for thinking of me! That's so nice of you." Or, "I appreciate the opportunity. It was so sweet of you to ask me first."

3. **Explain why you won't be attending, but be brief.** "I have a really busy weekend," or "I promised myself I would take some time to relax tonight." Sometimes no explanation is necessary, but if you're turning down someone close to you, an explanation is a nice touch.

4. **Show empathy.** Affirm that they're working hard or dealing with a challenging task. For example: "You're working so hard to help your sister plan her wedding. I wish I could take organizing the shower off your hands, but I just can't do that right now."

5. **Propose an alternative.** The huge birthday party may be overwhelming, but perhaps you'd like to catch up over coffee, just the two of you. Or, you can't help them write their resume, but you do have time to proofread it when they finish. Just make sure the alternative is something you actually want to do. If it's not, you may find yourself looking for excuses to back out when the day arrives.

6. **Don't budge.** Some people will pester you or ask more than once, hoping to wear you down. If this happens, it's okay to sound like a broken record. You don't have to be soulless about it. You can still empathize with them and propose an alternative. But don't let your "no" slide into a "maybe" and then a "fine, go ahead."

Put Solitude on Your Calendar (It's What Rock 'n' Roll Stars Do)

I recently had the pleasure of sitting down with introverted indie rocker jeremy messersmith. He's appeared on *Late Show with David Letterman* and has performed for former US president Barack Obama and vice president Joe Biden. *Time* magazine named him one of fourteen artists to look out for in 2014. He has a quiet yet powerful presence on stage, and his thoughtful lyrics are evidence of his deep-thinking nature.

Like all introverts, jeremy relishes alone time. And like many introverts, his love of solitude began at a young age. When he was a kid, he tells me, he channeled Superman and tacked a sign on his bedroom door that read "Fortress of Solitude" in an attempt to keep his siblings from intruding. As a teenager, he found himself alone at home for several days when the rest of his family went on vacation. His first move? He headed for the video store and rented dozens of movies, which he then binge-watched (there was no Netflix back then). "It was blissful," he tells me.

Today, jeremy travels with his band and performs for huge crowds of fans. But he still likes being alone. He uses his solitude to write new songs, play with new ideas, relax, and just be himself. "When you're by yourself, you don't have to do anything for anyone," he tells me. "You don't have to run any mental constructs. You don't have to run your 'spouse' algorithm, your 'American citizen' algorithm, or your 'musician' algorithm. You can just be yourself."

His wife, an extrovert, used to feel hurt when he wanted to be by himself. But jeremy has come up with a solution: he schedules regular, reoccurring alone time on their joint calendar. This prevents hurt feelings because his wife knows when he'll be missing in action. But it also ensures that he gets time to himself, because he and his wife can work together to protect his solitude by not scheduling other obligations at that time.

His advice to other introverts? Communicate about what you need. "For the longest time, I didn't know I could say I wanted to be alone," he says. "I didn't even know that was what I wanted."

Alone Time Is Not Personal Rejection

Brenda Knowles had just told her daughter that she would not be helping out with her third grade Valentine's Day party. "My daughter's eyes widened with hurt and confusion," she writes on her blog, *Space2live*. But Brenda just couldn't do it. "I had stayed home with her four out of five days last week when she was ill. There had been lots of bonding and mutual enjoyment. I had also been home for two days this week with her brother and his turn with the flu. I was taking them to History Day at the middle school [the next day]. Evenings are almost exclusively devoted to their homework and needs. I wanted the afternoon to myself. What I was failing to relay was the fact that my need for time alone was not a rejection of her company but a desperate need to explore my own essence."

Sometimes saying no to a loved one—like a child or a spouse—is the hardest of all. They may see your need for alone time as a personal rejection, even though you don't intend it to be. As a result, you may get in the habit of skipping solitude so you don't hurt anyone. But when you do that, both parties lose. You miss out on the recharging benefits of alone time, while your loved ones have to put up with a frazzled, half-present version of you.

Brenda has gotten better at explaining her need for alone time to her children. She makes sure they know it isn't about them. "I tell them it's how I'm wired," she tells me. "I told my children it's like being sleepy. If I don't get enough solitude, I crave it like an insomniac craves sleep. I can't help it." She also reassures her "significant people"—close friends, family, and her significant other—of a return time. "When I return after resting in solitude, I show them with my patience and renewed energy how beneficial that time away is," she says. "If I do not return energized, I know there is more than introvert depletion going on. For example, there may be conflict that needs to be resolved with a particular person."

Here are some more phrases to help you explain your need for alone time to your friends and loved ones:

- I really need some "me" time tonight.
- It's been fun, but I think I've had all that I can handle tonight.

- It's been a long day—I need some time to veg in front of the TV.
- Can we do it another time? I'm really due for a quiet night in.
- Would you hate me if I get out of here? I'm in desperate need of some time to unwind.
- I promise I'll be better company if we can save this for a day when I'm feeling livelier.
- I love when we get to spend time together, but I just don't have the energy today.

For Extroverts: Solitude Is Self-Care

To the extroverts reading this book: I get it. I get why you'd feel rejected when your best friend wants to stay home alone rather than going out with you on a Friday night. I understand why it hurts when your partner would rather play a video game than talk with you. It feels like personal rejection. I want to take a moment to absolutely assure you that it's not. It's simply self-care. Just like you may have needs to have new experiences, meet new people, and socialize, your introvert has a need to regulate their stimulation. Give your introvert some alone time, and you may be surprised at how attentive and energetic they are when they return.

Solitude Is Not *Hikikomori*

In Japan, there's a word used to describe young people who withdraw from society: *hikikomori*. These youths quit their schooling and jobs, hole up in their homes for months or even years at a time, and cut off all contact with their friends and families. They often describe themselves as feeling tormented. They want to do "normal" things like hang out with friends and date, but they're paralyzed by profound social fears. *Hikikomori* spend all their time inside, often within the small confines of their bedroom. They pass the time by watching TV, surfing the Internet, or sleeping the day away.

I'm telling you about the *hikikomori* because I want to make a distinction between restorative alone time and reclusion. The introvert's need for alone time is *not hikikomori.* Healthy alone time involves withdrawing from others for a little while for the purpose of getting re-energized. After a few hours, or at most a few days, it means returning to the world of people. If you find yourself withdrawing for very long periods of time and/ or cutting of all contact with others, I encourage you to reflect on why you're doing this. Consider reaching out to someone you trust who can help. You can live a better, happier life.

When Your Solitude Becomes Loneliness

For a few years after my divorce, I lived alone. On one level, it was wonderful. I had an apartment all to myself and more time than I'd had in over a decade. I would often lie on the couch for hours, just reading. Or I'd spend the night binge-watching my favorite shows in my pajamas. In moments like these, being alone was glorious.

However, there were other times when I was alone but didn't want to be. Because I divorced in my late twenties, most of my friends were busy with careers or were in serious relationships. I didn't have a lot of friends who wanted to casually hang out on a Saturday night. I was dating then, but as anyone who has dated can tell you, finding good company is hit and miss. On nights like these, I was painfully lonely.

As introverts, we champion our love of solitude, and we boast that we don't need anyone else to entertain us. But there's a shadow to this: for many introverts, solitude often becomes loneliness. Remember the 10 percent who responded to my survey saying they got *too much* alone time?

Along with making you *feel* miserable, loneliness can harm your physical health, too. Mounting evidence suggests that it can create high blood pressure, erode your arteries, and make learning and remembering things more difficult. Some research suggests that loneliness is even a predictor of an early death. That's because, whether introvert or extrovert, human beings are social animals. We evolved to need relationships to survive. We function at our best when our social need is met—whether that's having one close friend or three hundred. In fact, numerous studies have found that having strong relationships is crucial to living a happy, healthy life. According to *Live Science,* people who have high-quality friendships may cope with difficult situations better (like battling cancer or being picked on in school), have lower levels of inflammation in their bodies, and have a lower risk of high blood pressure than those who don't have quality friendships. For older people, having friends may protect against dementia; a 2012 study of people age sixty-five and older living in the Netherlands found that the lonely participants were 1.64 times more likely than the participants who didn't report feeling lonely to develop dementia during the course of the study. And having strong social ties may actually make you live longer. A 2010 review of research found that the boost you get from having quality friendships is twice as strong as the health benefit you get from exercising, and equal in size to the health benefit you would get if you quit smoking.

If you're an introvert who feels lonely, you're not alone. I encourage you to reach out to one person today. Just one person. If you're not comfortable having a face-to-face conversation, send them a text. You could also turn back to Chapter 5 and reread the tips about making more friends and having deeper conversations. Your health and happiness depend on it.

In Closing

When you're an introvert, solitude matters. It's the fuel for your mind and your very life itself. Without it, you feel worn out, mentally drained, and exhausted. You may lose touch with who you are and what you believe. Solitude isn't just about you, though. It's important to get enough of it so you can show up and be present for the people in your life. Most important, it creates the energy you can use to give back to the world.

Chapter 7

LET'S BE AWKWARD TOGETHER—
DATING FOR INTROVERTS

I walked into the noisy bar and immediately found the face I was looking for. He didn't look quite the same as he did in his dating profile (a little shorter, a little less muscled), but no one ever did. He recognized me right away, too, and I quickly became self-conscious. In what ways did I not measure up to *my* pictures?

He bear-hugged me and smiled warmly. Then came the small talk. "How was your day? What do you like to do for fun? Where did you grow up?" He fired off the questions, one after another, in rapid succession. I tried my best to keep up, answer quickly, and match his level of enthusiasm.

The night went on like this, and soon I became exhausted. My brain was no longer working. I tripped over my words. My sentences came out like molasses.

My date didn't miss a thing. "You've only had one drink!" he laughed when my speech slurred ever so slightly. And that was true. It wasn't the alcohol that was making me dumb.

I was on the verge of an introvert hangover. I was overstimulated by his high energy, along with the "newness" of the situation—a bar I had never been to and a person I wasn't yet comfortable with.

Eventually we said an awkward goodbye and left the bar. Soon after I got a text. "It got a little awkward at the end, didn't it? But I know you were tired. Let's get together again this Friday."

Still feeling self-conscious about his "awkward" comment, I flounced into the coffee shop on Friday, wearing a short pink dress. I was determined to be flirty and fun. This guy was everything I wanted, wasn't he? He was creative, interesting, and fun. He was a filmmaker who had built a successful business from scratch. And let's be honest. He was cute. *Really* cute. I wasn't going to let my introvert tendencies sink my chances with him.

We went to a nearby park, hiked around, and got ice cream afterward. I was having a good time, but just like on our first date, social burnout struck. When he dropped me off at my apartment, I bolted from his car and into the quiet solitude of my apartment, where I lay on the couch in silence, recharging.

This went on for several weeks. He wanted to hang out four to five times a week, and always at noisy restaurants, bars, or concerts. "I love being out of the house and *doing* things!" he told me. Often we met right after work, and our dates stretched well into the evening. Then I had to get up early the next morning for work and do it all over again. Each time we got together, I was always the one to call it quits and head home because I was tired. He started to tease that I "didn't know how to have a good time." Once, I got him to agree to a low-key dinner date at home, but he acted bored, as if he was just doing it to oblige me.

The relationship lasted for about two months before it fizzled out. In retrospect, I was never my best self on those dates because I was almost always overstimulated. The way my mind and body reacted on our first few dates should have been a clue to me that as much as I liked the idea of a relationship with him, it wasn't right. I needed someone who would not just tolerate a night in but relish it. Someone who would understand that we don't need to chatter constantly to stay connected. Someone whose words and presence would energize me, not drain me.

Don't get me wrong. I'm not saying that introverts and extroverts shouldn't be in relationships together. I've dated some extroverts, whose company I really enjoyed. I chose to share this story with you because it taught me a lesson I'll never forget: whether introvert or extrovert, the right person for me is someone I feel good being around.

If you're a single introvert who is dating, you hold a special place in my heart because I know what you're going through. I've suffered years of awkward first dates, flings that went nowhere, unrequited love, and serious heartbreak. On one hand, being single and dating was one of the most exhilarating and personally meaningful times of my life. I found myself growing and changing in ways I had never imagined as I met new people and had new experiences. But on the other hand, it was simultaneously the loneliest, most difficult period of my life. I worried that my introversion held me back. That I was too weird or quirky to be loved. That my high standards meant I'd be forever alone.

Many of the introverts I talked to when writing this chapter felt the same way. They worried that their introversion was more of a liability than an asset when it came to the dating game. If that's you, read on. You don't have to change who you are to find Mr. or Mrs. Right.

What Introverts Want in a Partner

What gets introverts going? To find out, I asked introverts to describe the qualities they want in a partner. I got over two hundred answers, and the responses were as unique as the introverts who gave them. But there were a few things I heard over and over. Introverts want someone who . . .

- Can hold a meaningful conversation with them
- Listens
- Respects their need for alone time
- Understands them and appreciates their quirks
- Is intelligent (a "meeting of the minds")

Here is what some of them said, in their own words:

"After being single for nearly three years following the very painful end of a marriage, I'm starting to feel ready to date again. I've dipped my toe into the online dating pool, though I am not particularly hopeful that I will find someone who can truly understand and appreciate me. The first time around, I feel like I had to present a certain side of myself—the more extroverted, spontaneous side—which is me about 25 percent of the time with lots of recharge time in between. My fantasy is to be with someone who can bring out that side of me while also respecting and cherishing my sensitivity and need for quiet and solitude."

—Claire

"I find myself being attracted to introverts. One reason is that introverts tend to have a calm energy, a peaceful core that is in sync with my energy. Some extroverts, when I'm around them, seem to have a more restless energy that runs counter to mine. Being around that kind of energy always makes me feel like I'm swimming against it as opposed to flowing with it. If you're an extroverted friend, I can handle it for however long we hang out. But having a potential partner possess that restless, extroverted energy might be too much for me to handle. Too much friction. Also, so much of what I value most about life is connected to my introversion: reading, writing, ruminating about various philosophical ideas, preferring a few close friends over many acquaintances—all seem rooted to the essence of who I am. And being with someone who doesn't get any of that and is the complete opposite would be difficult. That being said, I don't want a carbon copy of myself—that would get boring. I want someone to bring me out of my shell and expose me to new ideas and experiences. And certainly, extroverts can enjoy reading, writing, and other seemingly introvert-oriented activities. So I suppose it's just about finding the best match for you."

—Justin

"I'm all about inner qualities. I'm not focused on outward appearance. Since my focus is predominantly inward, I found someone who understands the mystery of my inner world. He has replaced what used to be my alone time with what I now crave instead—'us' time. I can be myself and not hide any of my introversion."

—Angelica

"I like deep thinkers. Someone whom I could have a next-level conversation with and who would not find it awkward."

—Taha

"Someone who puts in genuine effort into the relationship. Effort means a lot."

—Dean

"Kindness, above all. People who care deeply—about others, about their principles—are the most attractive people to me."

—Jessa

What qualities are on your list? If you're looking for a long-term partner, take a moment to think about what your significant other is like. But don't focus too much on qualities like *sense of humor, likes to travel,* and *is at least five-foot-eight.* Instead, put qualities like emotional stability, integrity, empathy, reliability, and agreeableness at the top of your list. Why? Because research suggests that the most happily married people are those who, regardless of what they *think* they want in a partner, simply end up with spouses who have excellent personality traits. In the long run, it may not matter that your date is carrying a few extra pounds or doesn't share your obsession with K-pop. If they're stable and cooperative, there's a good chance you'll be happy with your relationship decades later.

Why Dating Can Be Hard for Introverts

No matter what qualities you're attracted to, dating can be hard. And it's hard whether you're an introvert, extrovert, or whatever-vert. How do you meet people? What do you say? And what if you get rejected? Introverts face particular challenges when it comes to dating. For one, we probably don't put ourselves out there as much as extroverts. Most nights, we'd rather relax at home or hang out with just a few close friends. When we do go out, we don't have a huge desire to strike up conversations with strangers. Awkward small talk coupled with the fear of rejection? No thanks, I'll just get three more cats and be alone forever.

If you're an introverted woman, you face your own set of problems. The biggest one is that you probably don't fit gender stereotypes. Television and movies tell us that women are supposed to be flirty, forward, and fun. Think Rachel from

Friends and Gloria from *Modern Family.* These women are the embodiment of extroverted charm. They chat, they flirt, and, because it's TV, they look amazing while they do it. Comparing yourself to extroverts like these, you may feel less desirable and confident.

Likewise, if you're an introverted man, you may struggle with our society's expectation that you're supposed to make the first move. I interviewed Steven Zawila, who writes a dating advice blog for introverted men called *Charming Introvert,* and he says this is probably the biggest hurdle introverted men face. "We may struggle with being confident," he tells me. "We're expected to be the initiators throughout most of the relationship. It's up to us to ask her out the first time, to go for the first kiss, to ask her to be exclusive, to say the first 'I love you,' and so on. This can be terrifying because it means risking social rejection by someone whom you really care about."

If you're LGBTQ, you may face the above problems plus additional ones. For one, you may have a harder time than extroverts talking about your sexuality. Justin, who is gay, says he is private and tends to internalize everything. As a result, he wasn't open about his sexuality when he was younger. "I tend to overthink and overanalyze everything, and when I was younger, being gay was just one more thing I had to figure out and come to terms with on my own," he tells me. "And while that teaches resiliency, sometimes it's helpful to have another voice weigh in. Especially when yours is self-critical. So while I thought about myself and who I was all the time, I didn't always approve of the conclusions I arrived at. Maybe if I was less introverted and less introspective, and just more outgoing, social, and extroverted by nature, I would have found a friend I could confide in a lot sooner than I did."

Part of the problem was he didn't want to call attention to himself. "I knew this gay thing would make me the center of attention," he says. "So I kept it as buried as I could until I couldn't any longer. Being reflective, daydream-y, and introspective are admirable qualities, but when there's something toxic brewing within you, like the self-hatred that brewed in me, sometimes you have to expunge it and open up to someone else. That's not easy to do when you're an introverted kid already taught to hate yourself for who you are: a shy, quiet loner who clams up in front of strangers and prefers reading alone than playing basketball with the other boys." Even today, Justin, who is in his thirties, is choosy about who sees that side of him. "Though I'm not in the closest, I don't willingly discuss my sexuality except with close friends," he says.

Finally, no matter whom you love, you might know what this feels like: Everyone keeps telling you to try online dating, but you're hesitant because it feels inauthentic. You have an aversion to the superficial social interaction that it is sometimes characterized by. "I see online dating sort of like networking for a job," Justin says. "There's so much pressure to put your 'best self' forward and to be outgoing, smart, funny, etc. For an introvert like me who craves authenticity in social interactions and only feels connected to people when we're talking about our deepest dreams, hopes, and fears, there's something that rings hollow about online dating."

Are Introverts Too Picky?

Kate is twenty-nine years old and has never been in a serious relationship. "I meet people and realize they're just a little off from what I need," she says. So far, she's only ever met one guy who she really felt could be what she wanted—and, of course, he already had a girlfriend! "My family has told me many times that I'm too picky, but my best friend was able to put it another way: 'It's like you're looking for a thumbprint, and you'll just have to keep looking until you find the one that's just right.' Someday I'll find the right one."

Kat is another single introvert who is looking for a partner. She's picky—and she knows it. "Because when I was not, I ended up exhausted and unhappy," she tells me. But she's starting to doubt that she'll ever meet the right person. "It has been five years and I haven't met anyone I'm interested in. There are plenty of men out there but none have sparked me." Kat, who is in her thirties, says it's kind of painful to see everyone else coupling up and settling down. "So occasionally I have self-pity sessions, and I do not appreciate being different," she says. "However, I cannot settle for something that does not feel right. Only time will tell."

Have you ever been told that you're too picky about who you're willing to date? That you'll never find someone who lives up to your high standards? If so, here's some good news: Being selective about who you get into a relationship with can be a *good* thing, according to psychologist Rom Brafman. When you're picky, you avoid settling for someone who may not be right for you.

When people settle, they usually do it for one (or all) of the following reasons, writes Brafman in a *Psychology* Today blog post:

- Loneliness: "I want someone special in my life, and I'm tired of spending so much time alone."
- Time pressure: "Everyone else is getting married and starting a family—I'm running out of time!"
- Opportunity cost: "If I break up with him/her, I may never find someone better."

Each of these reasons is not a good rationale to date someone, because they're all based in fear. And when you begin making decisions from a place of fear, it's no longer about *who* you're dating but rather what you *stand to lose*. When you approach dating with a fear mind-set, you snatch up anybody who's interested in you, regardless of how compatible they are with you. I've been guilty of this. It's like drinking curdled milk because you're desperate for anything to quench your thirst.

Dating shouldn't be about finding someone who's going to "work." Instead, it should be about finding someone who mesmerizes you. Someone who excites you. Someone who you don't have to convince yourself to go out with. Being picky forces you to value yourself. It takes time and patience to find the right match, but it's one of those times when it's really worth the wait.

Debbie is an introvert who heard the "you're too picky" line over and over. "My friends always told me I would end up alone if I didn't give these 'good guys' a proper chance," she tells me. "I just couldn't get myself to settle even though I knew they were great guys." Even when she was lonely, she believed there was someone out there for her. "And thank God I did not settle because I found him, or rather he found me," she says. "He understands me completely even though he's an extrovert, and he accepts me completely." Now, happily in a relationship, Debbie has some encouraging words for other introverts who've been accused of being too picky. "I assure you, you are not being unreasonable," she says. "What you're looking for is not unobtainable."

A Caveat to Being Picky

I'd like to add one caveat to the "being picky is a good thing" idea. If you haven't done much dating—for whatever reason—consider this strategy: you could lower your pickiness shield for a time and go on a date with anyone you're even mildly interested in. That cute guy at your friend's birthday party who wants your phone number? Sure, why not. The attractive woman in your class who asked you to get coffee? It couldn't hurt. You can give anyone a first or second date—but you don't have to give them a third.

There's an important thing you have to do while on the date. Don't mess up this part. (I've messed this up and allowed relationships I just wasn't that into to continue for too long.) While on the date, notice how you feel around the other person. How does your mind, heart, and body react to them? Do they drain or energize you? Does your mind bubble with interesting ideas when the two of you talk, or are you bored? Are you physically attracted to them? Use your introvert super-powers to reflect on and analyze the date. Don't ignore the feedback you're getting from your emotions and body. Ironically, we introverts can be both highly introspective and hyper-tuned in to the people around us, but we can have a harder time discerning our own preferences and feelings—until we make a conscious effort to do so.

If someone doesn't excite you, don't keep going on dates with them. After enough dates with a variety of people, you'll find yourself becoming an expert on what you want and don't want in a partner. Better yet, you'll become an expert on *you*.

And there's a bonus: going on dates can help improve your social skills. You can treat each date as an opportunity to learn more about how these crazy creatures we call human beings work. See each date as a mini-workshop to refine your social prowess. For example, you might practice strategies to tame your pre-date anxiety, learn how to talk about yourself more comfortably, and figure out how to keep the conversation going by asking interesting questions. At the end of each date, ask yourself, "What could I have done to make the date even better?" Don't go overboard with analysis, but tap into your natural desire to improve and optimize things.

Remember how I wrote at the beginning of this chapter that dating was a time of personal growth for me? That's because I used this strategy. There were a lot of horrible, awkward date fails at the beginning of my dating "career." But as I added more experience to my dating resume, I found myself becoming more in tune with myself—and my dating game drastically improved.

When you feel you've gotten a better picture of the kind of partner you want to be with, raise your pickiness shield again. Start saying yes only to people whom you could really see yourself being with long-term. At this stage, you may have to pass over a lot of people—just be patient.

When You Get Too Attached Too Fast

Liz is an introvert who doesn't do casual. "If I don't have a great time with someone immediately, I move on," she tells me. "But there have been a few guys whom I really liked, but I become 'too much,' and I think I scared them off. Maybe I get too hopeful?" Liz was in a "dysfunctional but super connected relationship" for nine years. It ended about a year ago, and since then she's dated a few people but none have stuck. "I wish I could just 'keep things light' as people tell me and not get attached so quickly. Maybe it's because I know that connection doesn't come very often." She's getting to the point where she wants to give up and stop putting herself out there. "It's lonely, but at least I don't get hurt or disappointed."

Liz isn't alone. Many introverts have told me that they're just not into one-night stands, hookups, and flings. Casual seems too superficial, too meaningless. When they finally do find someone they're into—physically and emotionally—they fall hard and fast.

It isn't a bad thing to take dating seriously, especially if you're looking for a partner to settle down with. Everyone has to make their own call about whether one-night stands and hookups are right for them. (This is a judgement-free zone, no matter what side of the fence you're on.) Personally, I completely understand what Liz means about getting attached too fast, because I've been there, too. Once, I met someone whom I fell for almost immediately. Our eyes locked across a crowded room, just like in a movie. He was sitting at a table alone, looking tantalizingly introspective. What followed was a deep, meaningful conversation that lasted well into the night. Finally, someone who got me! It was the first time I'd ever felt such a strong connection with someone, so my thoughts became obsessive. All I could think about was him—even though I barely knew him. I know now that my fantasizing clouded my judgement, and I failed to see that he was not the right person for me. We had a strong emotional connection, but to be blunt, he was flaky and unstable. Even though he wasn't the partner I really needed, when our relationship fizzled out, I was crushed.

If you find yourself becoming obsessed with someone you barely know, proceed with caution. It's easy for introverts to idealize a potential love interest. Because we're so in our heads, we can be in danger of filling in the gaps with our imagination and become quickly attached to something that isn't even real.

When You Put Someone on a Pedestal

Something similar happened to Steven Zawila of the blog *Charming Introvert* a few years ago. He had a crush on a woman—let's call her Joyce. "She was stunningly gorgeous, and I really liked her," he writes in an *Introvert, Dear* article.

"She was always really friendly toward me." So Steven began to imagine the two of them together. He fantasized about being in a relationship with Joyce and having her as his girlfriend. "If I saw her and was able to talk to her, it made my whole day," he writes. "And if I went a few days without even seeing her, I became depressed—sometimes to the point of having trouble eating."

This went on for weeks, then months, and then over a year. "They say there are 'plenty of fish in the sea,' but I didn't want to hear it," he writes. In the whole time he obsessed over her, Steven didn't try to ask her out even once. "I knew that if I asked her out, there was a chance she would say no. And that would be impossible to deal with, especially after months and months of having become obsessed with her. It was easier for me to live in my fantasy world where the two of us were together then to face the reality that she may not actually want that."

Then one day, Steven learned that Joyce was moving away and that he'd probably never see her again. He finally decided to ask her out. "By that time, my expectations had become so high that there was no possible way she was going to live up to them," he writes. "I had put her on a pedestal, and no woman wants that. She said no and, naturally, I was crestfallen. That night I shut myself up in my apartment, and I cried myself to sleep."

Eventually Steven got over it, but that one rejection was a very tough pill for him to swallow. For months, he had pinned all his hopes on a single woman, which made him desperate around her. "Don't do what I did," he writes. "Don't put her on a pedestal."

For Extroverts: What You Should Know about Dating an Introvert

Are you an extrovert who is interested in dating an introvert? Here are some things about us that you should know:

We take things slowly. If extroverts are the hares, then introverts are the tortoises. Introverts tend to open up to new people more slowly than extroverts. We may not make a move as quickly (i.e., ask you out or get physical right away). Also, we may reach relationship milestones more slowly (i.e., saying "I love you" for the first time or proposing). That's because we like to think things through and carefully consider all aspects of a situation before we make a decision. We need time to process our experiences and reflect. Relationships are no exception.

We may have trouble talking about ourselves. Seriously. If we're on a date with you, especially a first or second date, we may stutter and fumble for words when you ask us about ourselves. Introverts are like onions—our personality has many layers, and it takes a while to discover them all, especially the hidden layers closest to the core. We're private, and we won't reveal the most personal parts of us until we fully trust you.

Want to truly connect with us? Talk about ideas or other meaningful topics. When the time is right, try asking some questions to take the conversation deeper. "What in your life are you most proud of?" "Do you have a dream or goal that you've never shared or thought was possible?" "Have you ever read a book that changed you?" Your introvert will probably light up.

We flirt differently. Think subtle moves, not bold. We might give you a sly smile. A gaze that lingers. Listening intensely and asking thoughtful questions. Revealing our secret inner world to you. What we probably won't do: aggressively hit on you or make overtly sexual remarks.

But I Don't Wanna Leave My House

Every time I see this meme on Facebook, I laugh. It says: "I found out why I'm still single. Apparently you have to go outside and let people see you." It gets a lot of likes and shares because there's some truth to it: it can be hard for introverts to meet potential partners because we don't socialize as much. How do you meet people when you don't want to hang out in noisy bars and crowded clubs? The good news is you don't have to. I mean, you'll probably still have to *go to places* and *talk to people*. But you can do this in a way that's more your style. Here are three ideas to help you meet potential dates:

1. **Through your hobbies.** Pick an activity you enjoy or you would like to try. Then find a place where there are other people doing that activity. For example, if you've always

wanted to learn to cook, take a cooking class. Or maybe you're the kind of person who loves helping people—so try volunteering (VolunteerMatch.org is a great way to find volunteering opportunities in your area). The people you meet at these events already share a common interest with you, so it will be easier to have conversations. People are more receptive to talking with a stranger at meet-ups than they are at a bar.

2. **Through your friends.** Ask your friends if they know anyone you might be interested in. Keep in mind that extroverts, by definition, love to surround themselves with people and tend to be very connected. If you have an extroverted friend, they may have several acquaintances whom you've never met. Having a "warm" connection helps break the ice and allows you to skip a lot of the initial awkwardness at the beginning of a relationship.

3. **Give online dating a chance.** I know, I know. Your friends and family have already told you this. And swiping through profiles feels more like shopping than falling in love. But online dating offers some advantages to introverts. It allows you to filter people based on their interests and personality type before you talk to them. And you can do it from the comfort of your own bedroom. Introverts, rejoice!

But I Don't Know What to Say

Like many introverts, Steven struggled with talking to the people he was interested in. "As introverts, we face a lot of pressure to be more like extroverts," he writes in an *Introvert, Dear* article. "Susan Cain, the author of *Quiet,* calls this the 'extrovert ideal.' For a long time, I always thought that something was wrong with me because of my introverted qualities and that women would never find me attractive. After all, one of my friends who I always saw getting dates had the opposite personality as I did. He loves to surround himself with people all the time. When he talks to women, he is very aggressive and makes the conversation overtly sexual very quickly."

That's not Steven's style at all. He describes himself as introverted, reserved, and gentle. "After watching my friend succeed seemingly all the time while talking to women, I started to become afraid that I would have to change my personality to be more like his if I ever wanted to get a girlfriend." For a while, he tried to behave more like his friend. However, he didn't get anywhere even though he was doing the same things his friend was. "I also started to feel like I an actor by going against my own personality," he writes.

What was Steven doing wrong? He quickly found out. "Women could sense that I was being inauthentic—and they were turned off by it." Here are three ideas from Steven you can consider so this doesn't happen to you:

1. **Be your best authentic self.** Or, in other words, be the version of yourself that your friends and loved ones enjoy being around. How do you behave around the people you are comfortable with, and what is it that they like about you? Try to be this person when you're talking to a potential romantic interest.

2. **Listen for what the other person is interested in.** Becoming a good conversationalist involves talking in terms of the other person's interests and listening to them when they talk about themselves. This shows you're interested in your date's values, experiences, and beliefs. You're interested in who they are as a person. And listening is something introverts often excel at. Try to find something that your date would enjoy telling you about. Remember to ask open-ended or "why" questions.

3. **Talk about the things that make you interesting.** If the other person is interested in you, they would enjoy learning more about you, too, and about what gets you excited. Are they asking you open-ended questions about yourself? This basically means, "I want to learn more about you." Tell them what makes you an interesting person. Do you have an awesome job? An adventurous story? Have you read something unusual recently? Introverts typically don't like talking about themselves, but this is one time when you'll have to push yourself out of your comfort zone a bit. You don't have to tell them your entire life story or reveal intimate, embarrassing details. But you should tell them enough to give them a sense of who you are.

Don't Fake Being an Extrovert

As you talk to people you're interested in, it's okay to be friendly. It's even okay to step a bit outside your comfort zone and push the limits of your gregariousness. But be careful not

to manufacture too much of an extroverted persona. Although it might be tempting to fake being more social than you really are when you're trying to attract a love match, eventually this approach will backfire. You may find yourself involved with someone who would have preferred being involved with an extrovert—and feels tricked into a mismatched relationship. Later on, you may find yourself resenting your partner's expectation to go, go, go, and talk, talk, talk.

Be yourself, and don't hide the fact that you're an introvert. People are drawn to others who are comfortable in their own skin. You may not be everyone's cup of tea, but that's okay. In the end, it will pay off because you'll attract someone who is interested in the real you.

How to Be Quietly Intriguing

You don't have to act like an extrovert to attract others; introverts can be intriguing in their own way. Here are some ideas from Michaela Chung, author of *The Irresistible Introvert*, to harness your quiet charisma:

- Express yourself authentically. Say what you really think and feel. Some introverts are afraid to say what's on their mind, so they stick to "safe" topics, never really revealing things that allow other people to get to know them better. Authentic expression provides opportunities for connection with the right people.
- When it comes to expression, a little goes a long way. "Luckily for introverts, this is one of those instances where less is more," Michaela writes. "We don't have to be over the top for others to take notice. In fact, our calm demeanor makes any form of expression that much more intriguing. I know a lot of people who go around expressing every passing thought and emotion. After a while, nothing stands out. All the words and revelations melt together like a really long run-on sentence."

- Own whatever state you're in. Let's say you are at a party and are tired of conversing. Try politely excusing yourself and stealing a few moments of solitude. As you perch on top of an overstuffed ottoman, watching the room and taking a voluntary time-out, something interesting happens. People become curious about you. They wonder, *Who is this person? What are they thinking about?* Michaela calls this the "power of the push." When you don't do what people expect of you, it creates intrigue.

- Own the room. Imagine that you're in a place you feel comfortable being in, like your own home. Notice how your body language, words, and posture changes.

- Stay present. Introverts' minds tend to leave the present moment and go wandering. This puts a vacant look on our faces, and people know we're not with them. To be more present, try to experience the moment through your senses. Delight in the smell, feel, look, and taste of what is happening right now. When your mind starts to wander, bring it back to the sensations of the moment.

Will I Ever Find Love?

As I spoke with introverts about dating and love, again and again I heard things like this:

"I'm ready to give up that love will find me."

"I can see finding myself at the end of my life, offering the same explanation for never successfully marrying that author Louisa May Alcott did: 'I never managed to fall in love.'"

"All I can seem to manage are unrequited loves for me or from me, but never with the same person at the same time."

"In the past two years, I have not meet anyone who I have been the least bit interested in."

"What kind of patience do I need to still believe that I will find that someone?"

Being a single introvert looking for love is hard. Every day, you may doubt yourself. Every day, you may feel alone. You worry that there isn't anyone out there for you. People tell you, "Don't worry; it will happen." But you're pretty sure it won't.

What you're feeling is real, and it's perfectly okay to feel that way. I felt that way for many years. Eventually I figured if love was going to find me, it would; but if it didn't, I would have to be okay with that (spoiler alert: it did). I'm not going to try to talk you out of your feelings. But I do want to share Becky's words with you, in the hope that, one day, the same will be true for you. Becky tells me, "I'm an introverted, intellectual, unemotional, cynical woman, which makes it very hard to find a complementary match. I need someone who is extroverted enough to help me do the talking and occasionally go outside my comfort zone, but not so extroverted that I get burnt out on social activities. I need someone who is intellectual enough to sustain my interest long-term and who won't be intimidated by my brain or the way I talk. Someone who is emotional enough to take the lead and share his feelings so that I'm comfortable sharing mine, which is hard to find in a male. Someone who will embrace my cynicism, but also counter it with positivity to keep us balanced."

Becky used to think a person like this couldn't exist. "But I did find one, and he even came with a dozen extra 'nice-to-haves,'" she says. "Before him, I found dating frustrating and unfair. It seemed like nothing would ever work out. At times, I became so desperate that I poured time and energy into a clearly dead-end relationship that didn't even make me happy. But now I'm so glad that I went through all that to find him at the end of it. Being alone is not always glamorous, but finding a real connection is worth it." She has some advice for introverts looking for love: "Follow your heart, listen to your brain, and it will all be okay."

In Closing

I'm happily in a committed relationship now. Like Becky, after years of dating, I tripped across a fellow introvert who had all the same fears about his relationship fate that I had. After late-night phone conversations that I never wanted to end and a dinner date in my apartment, I finally felt understood by another human being, and a real relationship was within my reach. The rest was history. I wish the same for you, too.

Chapter 8

LET'S BE QUIET TOGETHER—
INTROVERTS IN RELATIONSHIPS

Alex Lidnin immediately regretted her decision to sign up for the accelerated geology course. All around her, people were introducing themselves and, in her mind, forging friendships that would earn them reputations like "Easily My Favorite Student" or "The Cool Guy Who Can Talk to Anyone." "I remember the moment I realized a summer camping trip (also known as an easy credit class) might rank as one of the worst decisions I've ever made," Alex writes in an *Introvert, Dear* article.

Those two weeks were some of the most disparaging times of her college career. "I was essentially trapped twenty-four hours a day with fifteen people who hiked, camped, bathed, cooked, and most importantly *talked* with me," she writes. Despite being terrified at the time, years later, she says she's forgotten most of the awkward encounters that she's pretty sure were only awkward in her mind. "At least that's what I tell myself when memories of the most embarrassing ones keep me awake at 3 a.m."

Then, one night, something happened that changed her life. She was sitting near the campfire, trying to ignore the people around her and read, when someone sat in the chair next to her. "I reread the same paragraph over and over and my mind argued with itself about who was being ruder: me, for not putting down my book, or him, for thinking I would do so," Alex writes. Eventually, for reasons still unknown to her, she put down her book and started talking to her classmate. They ended up talking all night—as the sun set, as the fire died, and as, all around them, people returned to their tents. He was an extrovert, so Alex found it easy to hold a conversation with him. "Movies, music, books, anything—I only had to mention a topic I enjoyed and he would fill in the remaining space with excited words I could never seem to string together out loud." As the night went on, Alex found herself growing comfortable with "his loud but almost comically kind opinions on everything." When the only voices in the campsite were theirs, they walked to the river and talked until it became absolutely clear they would fall asleep right there if they didn't stop talking and go to bed.

Five years later, Alex and that extrovert are engaged. "Our home, our cat, our life—all of it built on the mutual understanding that I probably won't put my book down every time he wants attention," she writes. "But if he waits long enough, I'll think of something to say."

Alex will always be thankful for the extrovert who interrupted her reading. She wouldn't have signed up for that summer course if she had known how much interacting with other students she would have to do. But if she hadn't, she would still be going to concerts alone, wondering if there was anyone out there who shared her "insanely specific tastes." "Like so many of life's struggles, though, I made it through and maybe even came out on the other side with a little more strength and fight in me," she writes. "I'll forever be grateful to myself for trying something I didn't know I would succeed at, but mostly, I'm grateful to my extroverted fiancé who sat next to the shy girl in class and just waited for her to speak."

Like Alex, many introverts meet their special someone when they are tottering on the edge of their comfort zone. And like Alex, they realize that enduring the stomach-knotting, heart-pounding awkwardness ends up being totally worth it in the end. This chapter will explore the different stages of introverts in relationships. We'll explore why introverts make amazing partners and answer this question: Should introverts be with a fellow introvert or with an exuberant extrovert? The answer may surprise you.

Why Introverts Make Amazing Partners

Introverts are often stereotyped as closed, withdrawn, and even dull. This doesn't sound like it spells passion and romance, right? In truth, introverts can make amazing partners. We bring a lot of strengths to the table. For one, we tend to be excellent listeners. At our best, we try to understand what our partner is saying, and we think about where they're coming from before we respond. This can be helpful, because once words are spoken, they can't be retracted or easily forgotten, *if at all.* Introverts truly understand the power of words—including well-placed moments of silence.

Because we're often comfortable listening and observing in social situations, we're okay with giving our partner the stage. This relationship superpower is especially valuable if our significant other is an extrovert. While our partner holds court, we won't feel compelled to wrestle attention away from them.

The list goes on. Introverts can create homes that become sacred spaces to recharge, and we may have a calming influence on our partners. And you know that "meaningful interaction" thing? Being in a relationship with an introvert means you may experience more depth and intimacy than you ever have before. We're curious creatures. We like to dig deep and really figure out what makes people (or things) tick—and we'll likely apply our natural curiosity to *you*. Like an eager scientist studying a once-in-a-lifetime subject, we'll work to decipher your preferences, likes, and dislikes. You may feel more known, seen, and understood than ever before.

Finally, we may be the most low-maintenance partner you've ever had. We don't want or need attention twenty-four seven. When you love an introvert, you gain the freedom and space to be yourself.

Introvert vs. Extrovert, by the Numbers

Introverts can make amazing partners. But should they be with a fellow introvert or an exuberant extrovert? In other words, are you happier when birds of a feather flock together, or do opposites attract? To find out, I put together a survey and asked my Twitter followers to respond. I asked introverts if they were currently in a relationship with a fellow introvert or an extrovert (or in no relationship). I received 770 responses. The results were:

In a relationship with another introvert—27 percent (208 respondents)

In a relationship with an extrovert—26 percent (200 respondents)

Not currently in a relationship—47 percent (362 respondents)

As you can see, about half of the introverts in a relationship were with another introvert and about half were with an extrovert. Also, almost half were *not* currently in a relationship (47 percent are single vs. the 53 percent that are in relationships).

Then I wondered about how happy introverts are in these relationships, so I created a more formal survey. I asked introverts in relationships to rate their happiness level from 1 to 5, with 1 being "Miserable" and 5 being "Amazing! I couldn't be happier." I also asked them to identify whether they were in a relationship with an introvert or extrovert. What would you predict? Would you hypothesize that introverts are happier with a quiet companion or an extrovert who brings them out of their shell? Two hundred and forty-three introverts responded, and the results may surprise you:

The average "happiness score" for introverts in a relationship with another introvert—3.8 out of 5

The average happiness score for introverts in a relationship with an extrovert—3.7 out of 5

Wow! The "happiness scores" for introverts and extroverts were so close; there was only one tenth of a difference. It suggests that introverts can be happy being with either an introvert or an extrovert.

Finally, I wondered about who we *think* we'll be happier with. To find out, I asked single introverts, "What personality would you prefer your next partner to have?" The choices were introvert, extrovert, and no preference. Two hundred and twelve introverts responded. Here's when things got really interesting:

Introverts who would prefer to be in a relationship with another introvert—46 percent

Introverts who would prefer to be in a relationship with an extrovert—24 percent

No preference—19 percent

And 11 percent of respondents chose "other" and explained by saying they wanted a partner who is a mix of both introversion and extroversion (an ambivert), "someone who is mature," "someone who understands me," etc.

What do these numbers suggest? Introverts may *think* they'll be happier with someone like them, temperament-wise. But, taken with the data on happiness scores, it suggests that we don't always accurately predict what will actually make us happy. It means if you're looking for a partner, you shouldn't automatically rule out someone because of their temperament. If you're in a relationship, and you're wondering if the grass is greener on the other side (when it comes to introversion or extroversion), that may not be the case.

A Partner Who Understands: The Introvert-Introvert Advantage

The numbers show that introverts can be happy with a partner of either temperament. But a relationship with a fellow introvert is going to look very different from a relationship with an extrovert. Let's take a look at the perks and challenges of being with either temperament, starting with the advantages of being with an introvert.

Amy is a thirty-something-year-old introvert engaged to another introvert, Eric. "There are just so many great things about our relationship," she tells me. For example, when they first met and were falling in love, she noticed that she didn't feel drained by spending time with Eric. "I slowly realized it was because we were both giving each other space even though we were often in the same room." When they moved in together, this easy way of interacting continued. "When we'd get home from work, we'd both just relax into our introvert time for a while. I would read, watch TV, be mellow, and Eric would put on headphones and check stuff on his computer." Giving each other space wasn't something they ever talked about; as introverts, they were automatically on the same page. After some "alone" time, they would get up and make dinner and socialize with their roommate for a short time. Eventually they would go back to giving each other their respective space. "I love that dating a fellow introvert means never having to explain when you need alone time or closing the door to the bedroom and kind of shutting the world out," Amy says.

Brandon and Rachel are two introverts who have been married for over five years. They're happy they found each other, because they match each other's energy levels and interests for

the most part. "We both respect each other's time to decompress after a social gathering," Rachel says. Brandon adds, "Our activity interests often coincide. There isn't one person who's ready to read in bed and the other raring to go clubbing." They recently went on vacation to Puerto Rico. It was nice because, as Brandon says, "We both were fine with hanging out and chilling a lot rather than buzzing about and meeting people and seeing stuff."

There are other advantages, too. If you're dating an introvert, there's no running commentary. Meaning, your home may be a calmer space. Also, your quiet honey probably won't pressure you to socialize as much as an extrovert would. Instead, you'll have a companion for quiet fun. Think: long hikes, interesting philosophical discussions, or long nights on the couch binge-watching a favorite show. Extroverts may enjoy these types of activities too, but their appetite for them tends to be quickly satiated. After a night in, they're likely to want to get out and get social.

Challenges of Being an Introvert-Introvert Couple

Being in a relationship with another introvert isn't all Chinese takeout and your favorite Netflix shows. There are challenges, too. For one, your alone time needs don't always line up. "I often forget that just because I'm done recharging and focusing on myself doesn't mean that Eric is," Amy tells me. "I will just walk into his office and start talking, asking questions, etc., without recognizing that he might still need alone time."

Also, introvert-introvert couples may also risk isolation. "The more difficult one is a problem I think many introvert relationships have, which is that we very rarely go anywhere or do anything," Amy says. "We both enjoy being home and alone so much that we have to remind ourselves to go out and be good friends to others, or be good partners to each other." For example, on more than one occasion, Amy and Eric bought tickets to a concert they had both wanted to see, but when the day came, they quickly talked each other into skipping it and staying home. They just didn't feel like dealing with the noise, people, and traffic. "We very rarely go to parties or game nights because we'd rather get our energy back from our long weeks by spending time alone," Amy says. "We make lots of plans to go on dates and outings that we cancel if we've had particularly rough days as introverts."

Like Amy and Eric, it may be all too easy for you to blow off friends and stay in if there's already someone at home you can snuggle up to. But be wary of losing touch with your social circle. A partner can't fulfill all your social and emotional needs—that's why we also have friends. If nothing else, if your relationship doesn't work out, you'll want to have friends you can lean on. And, especially at the beginning of a relationship, it's important to bring your significant other around your friends. They'll have an objective view of your new beloved and may spot potential problems that you miss. One way you can combat social isolation in an introvert-introvert relationship is to take turns playing the extrovert: one of you takes charge, plans a date, and motivates the other person to go.

Likewise, in introvert-introvert couples, you may have to work harder to spend time together. Introverts tend to be independent; we pursue our own individual interests and make our own fun. This can backfire if you and your partner become so independent that your lives drift in opposite directions. One of you may have to step up, and once again, play the extrovert, drawing your partner back into your world.

Brandon and Rachel have challenges, too. "We sometimes need to go out of our way to give the other alone time," Brandon says. "I will sometimes go to the coffee shop for a weekend morning or afternoon, even if I wouldn't have otherwise done so, so that Rachel can have some alone time. Same goes for me getting my alone time, too."

Brandon can be charming and fun, but in typical introverted fashion, he's more subdued in groups. Rachel says, "It used to bother me how my older sister perceived my husband. At home, when it's just the two of us, we can be ourselves because we don't feel like we're being observed. However, at family gatherings, I can sense that my sister doesn't 'get him' because he comes across as quiet and serious. Turns out, he doesn't 'get her' either. It bums me that she can't see the way he is at home."

But perhaps the biggest problem with an introvert-introvert relationship is they have a hard time getting off the ground. Jef, an introvert who is engaged to an extrovert, says he's never dated another introvert—at least not more than one or two dates. "Maybe it's because I wouldn't know how to start a relationship with an introvert!" he tells me. "If I'm happily enjoying myself and my time, why would I approach an introvert who is happily enjoying herself and her time?"

Energy to Spare: The Introvert-Extrovert Advantage

Deirdre, an introvert, dated an extrovert named Jason for about a year. "The great thing about dating him was that he was *always* up for an adventure," she tells me. "All I had to do was suggest that we go do something, and boom, we'd go do it." For example, Deirdre loves ghost stories and pop culture. The History Channel had a documentary about the best Halloween hangouts in the country, and one of them was a massive Halloween store in Worcester, Massachusetts. She had always wanted to visit it, and when she told Jason, they jumped in his car and just drove down. No convincing or cajoling needed.

And there are more advantages to being with an extrovert. For one, your extrovert will likely come with a built-in social circle. This means there will always be plenty of friends to hang out with—and some to spare. And of course, being around an extrovert means *things will happen,* because extroverts tend to be action-oriented. They have ideas, energy, and a strong need to get out and be around people. You may find that your extrovert stirs you from your cozy introvert cocoon at home and gets you to experience life in a way you may never have experienced on your own.

Jef, the introvert who is engaged to an extrovert, says the best part of his relationship is that it keeps him from living in his own little bubble—and becoming a full-on hermit. "It's nice to have someone at your side who's always willing (eager, really) to start a conversation and keep it going," he tells me. "Take work events, something that I'd normally dread. My fiancée will always be the person who gets people talking and keeps the conversation going. I learn more about other people from listening to her conversations with others than I would otherwise."

Christy, who is in a relationship with an extrovert, told me something similar. "Extroverts complement introverts," she says. "They not only pull us out of spending too much introvert hermit time, but when we do go out in public with them, they can do more of the talking for us if we don't feel like it. So they can protect our energy some."

Finally, your extrovert probably won't be afraid to let you know what's on their mind. Extroverts excel at articulating their thoughts (sometimes *every thought* that crosses their mind, to the chagrin of their introverted partners). The good news is, with extroverts, there aren't guessing games. They don't expect their partner to read their mind, and they don't bottle up their feelings, like introverts sometimes do. If your extrovert wants something or is upset, you'll know.

Challenges of Being an Introvert-Extrovert Couple

There was a downside to dating Jason, Deirdre tells me—and you can probably guess what it was. "He loved parties," she says. "Of course, I never wanted to stay long at all. I always couldn't wait to get back to his place so we could snuggle and watch a movie."

Jef says something similar. "A challenge is negotiating alone time. I'm sure that if she had full control, our calendar would consist of back-to-back social events, every night of the week. Dinner with so-and-so on Monday, happy hour with friends on Tuesday, etc., etc. Over the past years, she's agreed that Sundays are off limits—they are my day to shut down and read the newspaper, make dinner, and not have anything planned. The plans are the challenge: if I'm going to be social, I prefer that it just happens—a pleasant surprise visit, not a planned 'on this Saturday we're going to do X with these people.' All that planning just leads to me trying to find some excuse not to take part in the event."

And extroverts don't just go out to meet friends—they often bring the social event right to your living room! "They may invite random people over and not tell you because they don't think it's a big deal," Christy says. "Which is kind of scary when you need alone time and have stuff to do at home—and you live together!" This need for alone time "may look lazy and boring to them."

Unfortunately, an extroverted partner won't inherently understand your need for alone time. They may even take your solitude as a rejection of them. And if your solitude is hurting them, you may feel your only option is to cut back on it. But this isn't a good idea, either, because you'll eventually become resentful of your partner. Without enough downtime, you'll become tired, worn out, grumpy, and foggy-headed, too. You may find yourself snapping at your partner, children, or others unexpectedly. Thankfully, to recharge your introvert energy (and your positive feelings for your partner), sometimes all it takes is an evening to yourself. Having a room of your own can help, too, especially if you feel comfortable closing the door.

Another challenge of being in a relationship with an extrovert is you may have to force yourself to speak up more. We introverts can be guilty of leaving others to read our minds and guess what we want. It's important that you articulate your needs, especially when you're in a relationship with an extrovert, who may not intuitively understand why you need certain things. Find a way to speak up that is clear yet loving.

For Extroverts: What You Should Know about Loving an Introvert

She was the one at the party hanging back from the crowd, but she wasn't doing nothing. From the look in her eyes, you could tell she was watching the scene and not missing a thing. When you talked to her, she didn't bore you with superficial chatter about her weekend—she actually had something meaningful to say. Or maybe he was the quiet guy in the cubicle next to you. You almost always had to start the conversation, but when you did, it was worth it. He was witty and smart (a little unconventional), and you knew right away there was something different about him. Regardless of how you met your introvert, one thing's for sure: his or her quiet strength drew you in, and now you're here to stay.

Whether you and your introvert have been on one date or hundreds, here are some things you should know about being in a relationship with an introvert:

Introverts don't like being the center of attention. So don't propose live on a Jumbotron during the big game or ask the servers to sing "Happy Birthday" in a crowded restaurant. You may look around only to find your introvert hiding under their seat!

We won't go to every single party, happy hour, or family get-together. If you're an extrovert who loves a party, this is something you'll have to accept and respect about us, because it's probably not something that will change. Of course, as a partner who cares about you, we will go to some social events—but we may want to leave early because we're "peopled" out. Remember, large crowds, busy environments, and socializing drain us because we have a less active dopamine reward system than you. Look for ways to compromise.

We may be sensitive to conflict. In fact, many introverts struggle to meet conflict head-on, because arguing can be overstimulating and stressful. We may bottle up our feelings and revert to people-pleasing behaviors to avoid disagreements, or we may shut down when an argument does erupt. Tread gently. Some introverts find it helpful to write about their feelings or to step away from the conflict for a bit to process things. Don't take it personally if we need a brief time-out.

A busy schedule with no downtime will poison us. A weekend full of activities is what dopamine-loving extroverts crave, but for us, it's often too much. Our internal resources get depleted, and we feel the need to retreat alone to a quiet space to recharge. Sometimes we'll want to be completely alone, while other times, we may enjoy having you join us in quiet solidarity.

Know that introversion and extroversion aren't all-or-nothing traits. In other words, most people don't fit perfectly into one category or the other. Just like you can have your quiet moments, introverts can also enjoy socializing. It's really just a matter of dosage. So don't intentionally leave your introvert at home while you go to gatherings because you think they won't enjoy them. Likewise, don't be surprised if your introvert wants to host a party. Introverts get lonely too, and being the host of a party is a way we can socialize on our own terms.

We want time with you. This means time with *you* and you *only*—no friends, family members, or kids around for a while. We may be quiet in groups, but we can be masterful at connecting one-on-one. We'll use this time to try to reconnect with you authentically.

Look for pastimes that feed both of our energy levels. Your introvert may not enjoy dancing in the club after a certain time, just like you might get bored after a low-key night at home. Find a happy medium. Browse stores, go on walks, travel together, play video games, or pursue different interests while physically in the same space. Discover activities that make both of you feel good.

When Love Doesn't Work Out

Whether you're in a relationship with an introvert or an extrovert, sometimes love doesn't work out. And this can be excruciating. "We relentlessly question everything about ourselves, and these questions can often be negative and purposeless," writes Aute Porter in an *Introvert, Dear* article. "Am I destined to be alone forever? Am I too shy? Was I boring? Am I too awkward?" If we're the one who got rejected (the dumpee, not the dumper), "self-esteem plummets to the deepest lengths. Usually we try to justify the situation as a way to get over the person once and for all, which never works. Inevitably, our negative questions reach a new low. *Oh man . . . what is wrong with me?*"

Introverts and extroverts often react to situations differently, and breakups are no exception. While extroverts may distract themselves from heartache by going out and being with friends, we may find ourselves withdrawing from others and spending more time alone in an effort to make sense of what happened. Also, we may take longer than extroverts to get back into a relationship; research published in the *Journal of Social and Personal Relationships* found that divorced extroverts were more likely than introverts to quickly remarry.

Did you just go through a breakup or divorce? Things may feel awful right now, and maybe you can't imagine life ever getting better. But take heart. Eventually, things *will* get better with time. It sounds clichéd, but it's true—time really is the ultimate healer. According to a study published in the *Journal of Positive Psychology*, 71 percent of young adults took about eleven weeks to see the positive aspects of their breakup. In other words, people started to get over the breakup in a little under three months. Of course, it's a little different when it comes to the end of a marriage. A poll conducted by a dating website for people over the age of fifty found that it took an average of eighteen months for a divorcee to feel "over" the split. Other studies indicate that it takes about a year to get through the really painful, negative stage that follows a divorce, and another three to five years to fully recover. Keep in mind that there are a lot of factors that influence the healing process, so your time frame may be similar or different—and that's okay.

The important thing is to start moving toward your healing—in a way that honors your introversion. Here are some things to keep in mind:

- It's okay to cry. Your feelings are natural and completely normal. If need be, cry until you run out of Kleenex. Crying can actually make you feel better—after a while. One study from the University of Tilburg in the Netherlands found that although participants didn't feel immediate relief, about 90 minutes *after* crying, they reported feeling better than before they had cried. It's not clear yet why the body works this way, but it could be because tears release endorphins, which are our body's natural painkiller. Also, tears that are the result of intense emotion release hormones that allow your body to clear stored toxins.

- When you feel ready, talk to someone in your inner circle about what happened. We introverts tend to keep our feelings and experiences to ourselves, but now is not the time to bottle up your pain. Researcher Matthew Lieberman and his colleagues found that even though it may not seem like we discover any new brilliant insights when talking to someone, simply naming your feelings with words like "angry" or "sad" can help. That's because talking about negative feelings activates the right ventrolateral prefrontal cortex, which is a part of the brain that governs impulse control. According to Lieberman, this seems to dampen down the response in the amygdala, which is the area of the brain responsible for fear, panic, and other strong emotions. The conversation doesn't even have to be deep and substantive (although that's a bonus); simply voicing your feelings and labeling them has this positive effect.

- Wallow, but only for so long. Set a time limit. Conventional wisdom says the mourning period should be half the length of the relationship, so if you dated someone for six months, you should take three months to heal. This time frame may not work for you, though, so choose one that's right. The important thing is committing to making positive changes in your life after the grieving period—even if you don't feel like it.

- Resist the temptation to check in on your ex virtually. Pulling up your ex's Facebook profile may seem innocent; you tell yourself you just want to see how they're doing. But it will probably do more damage than you think, especially if you see they've already changed their status from "in a relationship" to "single" faster than it took for you to get another box of Kleenex. Consider blocking or unfollowing your ex on all forms of social media so their updates don't show up in your feed. Even months later, when you've mostly gotten over it, coming across a picture of your ex looking cute and recoupled may be enough to ruin your day—or days (this has happened to me). The innocent update will likely launch you right back into tears, grief, and self-loathing.

- Some alone time will be good for you—it will help you process your thoughts and feelings, so take this time. But resist the urge to hole up at home for days or weeks on end. This doesn't mean you have to hit the bars and clubs (like your extroverted friends may be urging you to do). Instead, try getting outside. Walk your dog, hike, or bike. Take photos of the changing fall leaves or glittering snow. Find a park bench in the sun and read a book. Being in nature can help reduce stress, and sunlight and exercise are instant mood boosters.

Being Single Can Be Awesome, Too

What happens when you don't want to be in a relationship? For many introverts, being single is a deliberate choice. Some can't imagine sharing a home with someone else. Others don't want a relationship to encroach on their work, hobbies, or alone time. Still others have met their soul mate, married, and even raised children with them, until they passed away—and they're not looking to replace what they once had.

Choosing the single life can actually be pretty awesome—and a lot of people do, according to Eric Klinenberg, author of *Going Solo*. Nearly 50 percent of adults in the US are single, and 32.7 million—roughly one out of every seven adults—live alone. Although there are no statistics on this, I'd be willing to bet that a lot of single adults are introverts. That's because there are pretty great benefits of being a single introvert. "There is a lot more independence when you're single as you rely more on yourself than you would if you were in a relationship," Dean, an introvert, tells me. "There is also less chance of drama and conflict." For Lance, it's about freedom. "You can do what you want when you want," he says. Renato says the best part of being single is "not having someone expecting your attention when you just want to be alone." For Lora: "My house is a quiet drama-free zone. I guess it boils down to being able to be me and not having to apologize to anyone for loving my life as it is." Finally, Kashya says what's great about it is "not having to put in the effort to be 'on' all the time."

Research shows that the benefits of being single are real. According to Klinenberg, singles have been found to volunteer more, have more friends, go out more in their neighborhoods, and even have the potential to go much further in their careers than people who are married. So whether you're choosing to go solo as a permanent lifestyle or as a temporary measure, take heart. Being single can bring good things your way.

If you're single, you likely have plenty of time and energy to focus on yourself. If you haven't already, reach out to interesting people in your life and cultivate more friendships. Having strong, close platonic relationships will remind you that you're never truly alone. Also, spend your free time doing things that you enjoy. "Whatever it is you love doing, go do it," writes Amelia Brown in an *Introvert, Dear* article about being single. "Being in a relationship can sometimes prevent us from spending our free time the way we want because we make compromises for the person we love. Being single gives you the freedom to do whatever you want. Take advantage of your free time. When you do get into a relationship again, you'll be glad you went on that road trip or took that cooking class. You'll have more confidence in your own abilities and have new, exciting experiences to talk about."

In Closing

Introverts can make incredible partners. When we do fall in love, it's intense, because finding true connection doesn't happen often for us. But as much as we love our partners, we probably won't show our feelings in the typical extroverted way. We probably won't gush, cry tears of happiness, or tell everyone we know about our new SO. You'll see our love in other ways: an understanding glance, a thoughtful love note, or a compliment whispered in your ear before you fall asleep. Or something less romantic, but extremely useful. Something that will make our partner's life a little bit easier. For example, one morning, my introverted boyfriend proudly announced that he had mapped out a route that would shave three minutes off my commute to work. When I responded with nonchalance, he gently reminded me, "This is how I show my love."

Chapter 9

TROUBLESHOOTING YOUR RELATIONSHIP

He tentatively reaches across the bed with a warm gentle hand—and Brenda Knowles recoils. "I just need a few more delicious moments of morning mind. I need that gauzy, thought-weaving space of nourishing idea play where I breathe fully and smile involuntarily. I need that space where I belong solely to myself," she writes on her blog, in a post called "I'm Sorry I Hurt You in Order to Save Myself: What Introverts Feel but Don't Always Say."

He rolls away from Brenda, stares at the ceiling, and blinks back rejection. With a sigh, he heaves himself out of bed and walks away. *I am so sorry*, Brenda says in her mind. *I can't give to you right now. I'm so sorry.*

The above scene is from the end of Brenda's marriage. "I appear selfish and cold, but what you don't know is that at that point I was so raw and overstimulated from years of exposing my introverted nature to the harried, competitive demands of externally-driven living that I couldn't bear the softest touch of a lover's hand," she writes. "I spent my days tending to the intermittent needs of three children, a house with never-ending upkeep, and the demands that come with integrating into a community."

Brenda felt like she could never slow down, because no one else did. "I had to thoroughly care for everyone and everything," she writes. "I was desperate for permission to go internal; to slough off the scabs and injuries from unnatural striving—and become smooth again." Brenda felt numb and anxious all the time. She had trouble getting out of bed. Her husband didn't know how to fix things, and neither did she. Eventually, the tension between Brenda and her husband reached a breaking point, and they divorced.

Today, things are a lot better for Brenda. She's writing, raising her children, and helping introverts through the personal coaching business she started. She spends a lot of quiet alone time in her favorite room of the house—her home office, which she calls her sanctuary. And she's dating again, too. "I've learned a lot about myself and how to love and be loved," she writes on her blog. "I love the relationship adventure."

Like Brenda, if you've ever felt the tug between your partner's need for togetherness and your need for space, you're not alone. In this chapter, we'll explore and troubleshoot some of the problems introverts experience in relationships. My hope is that if you're currently in a relationship, you'll deepen and improve it after reading this chapter. If you're not currently with someone (and you eventually want to be), I hope this chapter will help prepare you for when that day comes.

Why Relationships Can Be Hard for Introverts

Unfortunately, romantic relationships aren't all deep conversations over wine. If you're an introvert, you know that relationships can be really tough—extremely painful, even. I asked introverts how being in a relationship challenges them. Here's what they said:

It can be hard to express yourself to your partner, share your feelings, and communicate what's going on in your mind. Jennifer tells me, "I don't share my feelings as openly as is expected. My feelings are private and mine to battle. This comes across as not caring. I handle aggression/anger differently. I don't talk about it. I shut down and reflect until I work it out in my head." Yarin sums up his struggles: "I have trouble letting her in."

You sacrifice alone time. And just because you're in an introvert-introvert relationship doesn't mean solitude is guaranteed or easier to manage. Eric, an introvert who is married to another introvert, tells me, "We both need quiet time and a little bit of interaction, but rarely the same one at the same time. I'm more introverted than she is, so I need more solitude, and she needs more interaction. Coordinating things to fulfill both our needs without draining us can be a challenge."

You may be conflict-avoidant. Many introverts are nonconfrontational. We just don't like to rock the boat. Nina tells me, "Even when I should be arguing or at least talking about it, I don't. Sometimes I just say, 'Okay.'"

You worry that your introverted ways will bore your partner—especially if your partner is an extrovert. Faye says, "I feel like I'm boring because I don't want to go out much."

Your need for quality one-on-one time with your SO may be seen as rude or clingy. Kristyn describes a difficult scenario with a boyfriend she had in college: "I had a boyfriend who lived with roommates. I lived in Rhode Island, and he lived in Boston for school, so on the weekends I would head up there to stay with him. His roommate thought I was such a bitch because I didn't want to sit in the living room with them. I wanted to stay in my boyfriend's room. I would tell my boyfriend, 'I'm not here for your roommate, I'm here for *you*. I want private time with you because I don't see you all week.' Thankfully, that relationship didn't work out."

Your partner mistakes your quietness for anger or unhappiness. Snow says, "My partner often thinks I'm angry when I'm just quietly contemplating things, and I forget to correct my resting bitch face."

Choosing the Right Partner

Perhaps one of the biggest problems introverts face regarding relationships is choosing the right partner. How do you know when someone is right for you? Better yet, can you know early on if someone is *wrong* for you?

Andre Sólo had the habit of getting involved with all the wrong people. "Some of my early relationships were with people who shouldn't have made it past the second date," he writes in an *Introvert, Dear* article. "Even when these relationships became toxic, I held out hope far too long. I wanted to believe they were the right person for me, at least partly because I didn't really know who else I could find."

Growing up, he had been socially awkward, so when it came to dating, he figured beggars couldn't be choosers. "I grew up as your stereotypical 'nerd,' and I didn't think of myself as handsome," he writes. "My self-esteem in my early twenties was somewhere between low and rock bottom. It should be no surprise that I wrote off the very idea of talking to the women I found physically attractive. Instead I was eager to get into any relationship that might come my way—and if I didn't really feel chemistry with the person, who was I to complain?"

One summer, he had a fling with a charismatic extrovert. "We had common interests and a shared sense of adventure, but a very different level of stamina," Andre writes. His social butterfly partner planned an event for the two of them almost every night of the week. "She never seemed to wear out, but for me, even just three nights of this was too much—I'd find any excuse to sneak off on my own. By the middle of the summer, I was so drained I felt like I'd been drugged."

After several experiences like these, Andre eventually learned what a healthy relationship looks like. He recognized patterns in how he had settled in the past. Today, he's in a relationship that's right for him.

Look for Red Flags Early

No one shows up to a first date with a warning label adhered to their chest. But if you're an introvert who is beginning a new relationship, you can look for red flags. Red flags mean you should proceed with caution; they *don't* necessarily mean you have to break up. But the bigger and brighter the red flag, the more of a clue it is that there may be trouble between you and your beloved down the road.

I repeat: it's *crucial* to look for red flags at the beginning of a relationship. That's because the longer you're in a relationship, the harder it is for you to leave when it becomes emotionally unfulfilling or perhaps even dangerous, explains psychologist Susan Krauss Whitbourne, author of *The Search for Fulfillment*, in a *Psychology Today* blog post. Think about it. Breaking up always sucks, but it's easier to leave someone you've dated for only a few months than it is to say goodbye to someone you've been committed to for years. If you have a house and kids together, it's even harder to disentangle yourself.

Plus, it may be more difficult for introverts to leave a relationship than it is for extroverts. We may hesitate to act, getting stuck in analysis paralysis, spending weeks (or years) analyzing our situation. Because we tend to go out less and meet fewer people, we may worry that we'll never find someone else to love us again. This fear can trap us.

And, when you look for red flags, it forces you to make a conscious choice to enter a new relationship. The more effort you put into the decision to get involved with someone in the first place, the harder you'll work to keep the relationship strong, according to Whitbourne. Even if you decide to ignore red flags and enter a relationship with someone new who might be risky, you'll still be better prepared to deal with future problems. For example, think about how you would make the decision to buy a house. You may realize that it has some weaknesses (only one bathroom, needs a paint job), but you decide to purchase it anyway, accepting it for the trade-offs it brings. You may find that you work even harder to make it a space you truly enjoy, especially if you decide you're happy with it. It's the same with relationships; the fact that you commit to putting the effort in—despite your partner's imperfections—can make all the difference.

Red Flags Introverts Should Watch Out For

This is not a comprehensive list, but here are some crucial red flags introverts should watch out for:

Your family or friends don't like your new boyfriend or girlfriend. Other people are often able to see your new special someone more objectively. If you're getting lots of negative reactions from people whose opinion you trust, consider listening to them.

The relationship is moving too fast. Your sweetheart wants to make commitments before you're ready and pressures you to respond in kind. Lasting relationships start out more slowly.

The object of your affection has few (or no) friends. Introverts tend to have small social circles, but that's not what I'm talking about here. I'm talking about someone who doesn't seem to be able to tolerate other people in their life or get close to them. This could signal that your partner lacks the capacity for true intimacy.

Your SO doesn't respect your need for alone time. It's a constant battle to get a few hours to yourself. A partner who is clingy or needs constant attention will not be a good fit for an introvert in the long-term.

You often find yourself giving in to your partner's demands in order to avoid a fight. Another night out with friends, even though you don't have the energy for it? *Oh, okay.* This dynamic will lead to a life of perpetual exhaustion and resentment.

You don't get enough one-on-one time with your partner. Friends and family are always coming along for the ride. When you raise this concern to your partner, they accuse you of being needy.

You find yourself frequently saying "everything's fine" when it's not. You walk on eggshells and don't feel like you can express your concerns to your partner. You worry that speaking up will erupt in a nasty fight.

Your SO does not make contact with your inner world. You don't feel comfortable opening up to them, so you keep your most authentic thoughts and feelings to yourself. As a result, they don't know the true you. If they could see inside your mind, they'd be shocked.

You frequently feel lonely, even though there's another person around. This means the relationship is not serving your emotional needs. People feel lonely when they want to connect with someone, but no one is available or willing to connect. You will eventually look elsewhere to get your emotional needs met.

Your beloved is super secretive about your relationship on social media. Introverts tend to be private. We may not share all the details of our personal lives online. But if your partner posts with the frequency of a Kardashian and doesn't say a word about your relationship, it raises a red flag. If the two of you are committed to each other, and they're still hiding their relationship status or never posting couples photos, they may want to appear to be unattached. Couples who are excited about their relationship usually want to share their happiness with family and friends, at least on some level.

Your partner is your harshest critic. It's one thing to tolerate playful jokes and teasing, but if moral support is in short supply or if nitpicking and criticism are around-the-clock, it's a sign of trouble.

Your partner is a heavy substance or alcohol user. A pattern of getting drunk or high suggests that your new love may be dealing with deeper psychological issues that may continue or get worse with time.

Remember, none of these red flags alone are deal breakers. Just because you see a red flag doesn't mean you have to leave the relationship. But you should think carefully before proceeding.

Signs You're in the Right Relationship

How do you know when you've found the *right* relationship? It took Andre years to figure this out. Here are five signs you're in the right relationship, from his *Introvert, Dear* article:

1. **You're physically attracted to the other person.** It might seem strange to start off with something that's only skin deep. But physical attraction is an important part of a healthy romantic relationship—and it may get overlooked by introverts. Introverts tend to be deep-thinking and creative, so we may look for a partner who checks our intellectual boxes. This is great, but love can't survive on a shared reading list alone.

   Physical chemistry is part of what keeps couples together. If you don't feel physical attraction from the beginning of a relationship, psychologists say you're unlikely to ever develop it. Sadly, this can cause a relationship to fail, because a lack of chemistry will likely carry over to the bedroom. Sexual dissatisfaction with a partner translates to higher divorce rates for married couples and even higher breakup rates for unmarried couples that live together.

   Physical attraction means something different for everybody. Neither you nor your partner have to conform to society's standard of beauty to be happy. But if you are beautiful to each other, it's going to make your relationship happier and longer lasting.

2. **In general, you feel energized being around them.** This is a common plight for introverts. People wear us out, some people more than others. But every introvert has met a rare

individual who actually left you feeling energized. This is often someone who understands you, gives you time to express yourself, and is happy to meet for low-key, one-on-one activities. This kind of person can be an introvert or an extrovert. When you first start dating someone, ask yourself: how do you feel after you see them? If you feel energized and wish you had more time together, it's a good sign.

3. **Your relationship is rich with meaningful interaction.** Introverts don't like small talk. Unfortunately, that's what counts as conversation in some relationships. Every relationship will have some amount of it, from first date chit-chat like, "Where do you work?" to routine prattle like, "How was your day?" The problem is when that's the majority of the communication between you and your partner. If deeper, more meaningful conversations don't interest them, you may find your relationship unfulfilling.

   That's not to say that every meaningful interaction has to be spoken. Couples bond and connect in many ways—from playing video games together to cooking dinner for each other or creating special outings or date nights. Strong couples develop their own unique traditions and private jokes together. These are especially important for introverts because we tend to make a few deep connections, not lots of shallow ones, and we count on our partner to be one of them.

4. **You have a sense of mutual respect.** Respect is a bedrock of all relationships, but it's rarely mentioned when people describe their dream partner. Respect is very different from love. Both are positive sentiments, but respect

means admiring the person for their qualities and abilities. You can respect someone even when you're not happy with them, and the power of that respect can get a couple through the most difficult fights. Psychologists say that in some cases, respect may be even more important than love for a relationship to survive.

There's a lot of power in checking whether you feel respected in a relationship. There's also power in only dating people that you deeply respect. Ask yourself: would I look at my partner with admiration, even if I wasn't romantically involved with them? If the answer is yes, then you likely have a very healthy foundation for your relationship.

5. **Your partner doesn't make you feel guilty about spending time by yourself.** This one is huge. There's simply no substitute for having good, healthy alone time to recharge yourself as an introvert. Some partners get that, but others don't. And this isn't necessarily an introvert/extrovert divide. Some introverts are more social than others, and some extroverts will understand your needs—or they'll learn with time. But not everyone is adaptable.

Conflict Is Normal

Conflict in a relationship is inevitable. Normal, really. Chances are if you and your SO aren't arguing occasionally, either one or both of you are avoiding conflict. This tends to happen with introvert-introvert couples. Rather than making a big deal out of an issue, introverts might sweep it under the rug. But this can lead to resentment, passive-aggressiveness, and worst of all, a deterioration of intimacy. Eventually you just don't *enjoy* being with your partner anymore.

Arguments don't have to jeopardize a relationship. In fact, conflict can actually bring you closer together as a couple. It's all about how you and your SO decide to handle disagreements when they arise. Psychologist John Gottman, a leading researcher into why marriages succeed or fail, found that how a couple handles conflict is a good predictor of the relationship's long-term potential. If you can figure out how to fight fairly, you and your beloved have a good chance of sticking together.

Couples who have poor conflict management skills typically fall into the pattern of Fight, Flight, or Freeze behaviors, according to Preston Ni, author of *Seven Keys to Long-Term Relationship Success*. When they "fight," they remain hurt and angry, sometimes holding grudges for years. When they take off in "flight," the couple flees from addressing important issues—they ignore problems, hoping they'll resolve themselves on their own. Or, after countless arguments with no cease-fire in sight, they "freeze" emotionally and shut down. This is when things get really bad. Someone who freezes in a relationship may go through the motions on the outside, but they no longer care on the inside. Has something like this ever happened to you? It's happened to me.

Successful couples have the ability to solve problems and let the issue go. Instead of attacking the other person, they focus on taking care of the problem. Even when they're mad at their partner, they find ways to stay close—like seeing humor in the situation. When the fight is over, they forgive and forget. Most important, they use conflict to learn more about themselves and their partner, and grow the relationship.

Introverts Fight Differently Than Extroverts

Introverts tend to approach conflict differently than extroverts. An extrovert may want to deal with an issue immediately and head on. Out spews a torrent of words and emotion. Introverts, on the other hand, may need time to process when they're hurt. They may withdraw initially, rather than fight. They need time and space to think about what happened.

Neither style is better than the other. But problems can happen when partners don't understand each other's conflict styles. For one, in an introvert-extrovert relationship, the introvert might be overwhelmed by the extrovert's intense and sudden venting. Like a deer in headlights, the introvert may shut down. To make it all just go away, they may give in to whatever their partner wants. ("Okay, okay, I'll come to the birthday party with you! Can we just let it drop?") The extrovert goes ignorantly on their way, thinking they've won. Little do they know that their victory was false—and they've planted the seeds of resentment in their partner's heart.

Another thing that might happen is the introvert internalizes their pain. They never bring it up, instead turning to secret brooding and stewing. (I'm often guilty of this.) Their partner has no idea they've crossed a boundary, so they ignorantly do it again and again. Eventually the introvert snaps. ("I hate how you immediately point out everything that's wrong with my idea when I'm excited about it! What's wrong with you?!") Their partner is taken aback because they had no idea that the introvert felt this way. But to the introvert, the pain is very real. It's been festering for days, weeks, or even years.

Finally, partners may resort to passive-aggressiveness. ("No, I'm not mad. I just wish you could think about *my* needs for once.") Like I said, this tends to happen with introvert-introvert couples. Because neither wants to talk about the issue, they ignore it, hoping it will somehow just go away. But relationship problems rarely just disappear. Rather, they rear their ugly heads again and again until the issues are addressed at their roots.

How to Handle Conflict Better

How do you avoid screaming at your partner and/or shutting down? It's not easy, and it takes practice. Here are some tips to help you handle conflict better:

- Discuss your conflict styles before you find yourself in the middle of a fight. Are you an introvert who needs time to reflect and cool off before you can have a productive conversation?
- Don't let conflict fester. It's okay if you need a time-out. But your time-out shouldn't be an excuse to never deal with the issue. When you're ready, you have to make an effort to resolve it. Problems, offenses, and hurt feelings usually grow bigger if they're left unattended.
- Make an "appointment" to talk. When you have an issue with your partner, first ask them if it's okay to talk about it. Don't just launch into it. This is especially important if your partner is an introvert. Introverts do better when they have time to mentally prepare for things. Try, "Is now a good time?"
- Complain, don't blame, urges Gottman. No matter how at fault you think your partner is for leaving a mess in the

kitchen, hurling accusations and criticisms is simply not productive. It's all about the approach. Instead of blaming your partner by barking something like, "You said you would clean up the kitchen after baking cookies, but it's still a mess," try a simple complaint: "Hey, there is still flour all over the counter and dirty dishes in the sink. We agreed you'd clean it up. I'm upset about this." When you avoid lashing out, your partner is more likely to consider your point of view—which ultimately means you'll have a better chance of getting the results you want.

- It's easy to become entrenched in your side of the argument. It's like you get blinders on and you become convinced that your way is the only right way. But your partner has their side of the story, too. To combat single-mindedness, try activating your empathy. You can do this by pretending to be your partner. Think about how they might be feeling right now, and how the situation is affecting them. Then describe out loud how you think your partner is feeling. Your partner can respond by either agreeing or clarifying how they feel.

- Be specific about what you need or want. Ask for what you want in one or two sentences. Make it positive. Instead of, "I wish you could be on time," try, "The next time you're going to be late for dinner, I'd like to know that you'll call me and let me know."

- Show your appreciation for your partner. For example, you might say, "Thank you for listening to me." Or compliment your partner. Focusing on each other's positive attributes will remind both of you why you fell in love in the first place. It also helps to bring healing after things have gotten nasty.

- Conflict is a normal part of relationships, but it shouldn't be the background music of your relationship. If you and your partner are constantly fighting, consider seeking professional counseling. A trained professional can teach you both to fight more fairly.

About Those Pesky In-Laws

If you're married or in a long-term committed relationship, you know there are more people involved than just the two of you. There are family members or in-laws, and sometimes those in-laws are not introvert friendly. This can put a real strain on the relationship.

Yvette is married to a man whose family is very extroverted. "They are *loud* when they all get together, and between the loudness and the sheer numbers, it was (and can still be) kind of overwhelming," Yvette tells me. "They are not shy about sharing their opinions, and they enjoy talking much more than I do. They have often thought I am rude because I don't hang out and talk for hours and hours. It's not because I don't like them (I do!), but I can only take so much 'togetherness' before I need a break to recharge." And they don't understand this. "During our engagement, my future mother-in-law told me I was the coldest person she had ever met. Ouch. That one still stings a bit. We have come a long way since then, but she has never really understood my personality."

Sometimes Yvette feels bossed around by them. This started early in their relationship—at their wedding. In typical introverted fashion, Yvette wanted to keep the wedding small, but she felt railroaded into inviting all the relatives from her husband's side of the family, most of whom she didn't know. "I did invite everyone to please them, and it was fine, but it made me realize early on that I would have to put my foot down about things that are important to me," she says.

Lori has had similar problems. Her husband's family "is generally always talking . . . all at the same time," she says. "It's exhausting." She often worries that if she doesn't show up to every family gathering—and look enthusiastic the whole time—they'll take offense. Sometimes she wears herself out trying to make them happy.

Yvette has learned to take a firm stand on things that matter to her—even though she doesn't normally act that way. "I've had to learn to be pretty blunt in my communications with them, because otherwise they don't get how I feel," she says. And she's made peace with the fact that she'll have to skip a few family events or leave early, for her own sanity. It's a "healthy" type of selfishness.

If you have pesky extroverted in-laws, remember that ultimately you don't need to get anyone else's approval to live your life the way you want. And you may have to be assertive when it comes to getting your needs met. Of course, your initial attempts to communicate with your in-laws should be courteous. However, the problem with being too polite (for fear of coming across as rude or domineering) is that you don't express how deep the problem is, and how upset you are by it. This can lead to a lack of vital boundaries. In other words, it's okay to be kind—but don't let your desire for politeness dilute your message.

In Closing

For me, when my close relationships go well, my life goes well. But when something turns sour—a fight with my significant other, for example—I find myself quickly becoming unwell. I have trouble sleeping. Angry thoughts distract and poison me, stealing my happiness and productivity. My introverted nature tempts me to bottle up my thoughts, but I'm learning the keys to getting them out in a fair, productive way. And I'm learning to be more assertive about my own needs, like Yvette. You can, too.

Chapter 10

DO I REALLY HAVE TO DO THIS AGAIN TOMORROW? INTROVERTS AND CAREER

Kayla Mueller, an introvert, was sitting at her desk at work, bent over papers spread across her desk. She was concentrating deeply, like introverts tend to do. "When I focus on something, it's like my entire brain dives deep into whatever ocean I'm exploring," she writes in an *Introvert, Dear* article. "I can't multitask because to do that is to keep the brain only shallowly invested so that it can easily switch from one pool to another. My brain does not do this. It is all or nothing."

As she sits there, her extremely extroverted coworker walks into her office and fires a question at her. "I drag my eyes up like molasses sliding from a can, and she stands there, staring at me and waiting for my answer," Kayla writes. "My brain is still swimming back from the ocean, so I am not even sure what she asked yet. As my brain finally reaches the surface and takes a deep breath, her question hits me. It is simple, and I know the answer, but I'm not there yet. My brain is still in the water, eagerly searching for the dry land of another topic."

Kayla's coworker stands there, impatient. So Kayla tries to give her something: "Yes, er, no—wait, yes." Her coworker raises an eyebrow and snorts a small laugh.

Eventually Kayla is able to rattle off the full answer, and her coworker leaves, giggling to herself. "Because of her talkative, gossipy nature, she will probably tell everyone about what just happened," Kayla laments. "How she asked such a simple question, and yet I stared at her, dumbfounded."

Kayla has no disability or mental impairment. In fact, she received a scholarship to attend college and graduated with honors. The only thing that's "wrong" with her, she writes, is that she's an introvert. An introvert who needs time to think and reflect before answering.

"Why, then, do I constantly get these muffled giggles, pointed questions, and judging looks?" Kayla wonders in her writing. "My coworkers and others around me see something different. They do not see the thoughts running through my brain, the padlocks being opened to pull out old memories, or the little lightning bolts that send new information to my sensors while I wait to see what it all means. The only thing they see is me sitting there with a blank expression on my face." So, nearly every time, they jump to the wrong conclusions about Kayla. "They assume I don't understand what they're talking about or that I'm a little slow."

Have you ever felt like your introvert skills are undervalued at work? If so, read on. In this chapter, we'll explore the strengths of introverts on the job, as well as how you can choose a job that plays to those strengths.

Why More Companies Should Hire Introverts

Introverts can make seriously awesome employees and leaders, whether it's in the office, factory, store, boardroom, or classroom. For one, our penchant for working alone empowers us to solve problems and come up with unique ideas. We're the ones quietly sitting at our desks, turning ideas over and over in our mind, rather than clamoring to make our voice heard in a noisy conference room. And there's a benefit to this. When you're alone, you can clear your mind and focus your thoughts, and all this deep, concentrated thinking can lead to novel solutions and brilliant ideas. So, forget the brainstorming session—they may be overrated, anyway. According to Keith Sawyer, a psychologist at Washington University in St. Louis, research has consistently shown that brainstorming groups think of far fewer ideas than the same number of people who work by themselves and later combine their ideas, he tells the *Washington Post*.

Speaking of problem solving, we introverts are persistent. We tend to stick with problems longer—well past when everyone else has moved on to another topic or gone home for the day. Albert Einstein, the brilliant physicist who developed the theory of relativity, was probably an introvert. He's widely quoted as saying that while he didn't think of himself as a genius, the secret to his success was that he simply stayed with problems longer than other people did.

And don't think that introverts can't work on a team. In fact, research shows that quiet, neurotic introverts make *better* team players than extroverts in the long run. Corinne Bendersky and Neha Parikh Shah found that while extroverts make great first impressions, they may disappoint us when they're a part of a team. Bendersky and Shah conducted two studies, one that surveyed employee behavior toward extroverts and neurotic introverts, and another that noted MBA students' behavior. They found that the perceived value of extroverts' work and their reputation among their colleagues actually diminished over time. In other words, bosses often have high expectations for extroverts because they are enthusiastic, outgoing, and assertive; however, extroverts may not live up to these expectations. Plus, Bendersky told *USA Today*, the extroverts they studied were often poor listeners, and despite their drive to be social, they didn't collaborate well in practice.

Introverts, on the other hand, particularly those who score high in "neuroticism" on the Big Five scale, may be the better employee in the long run. Although neuroticism is often associated with anxiety, negative emotions, and irritability, people who are neurotic also tend to care a lot about what others think of them. This means they may work harder on a team because they worry about how their colleagues perceive them, and they don't want to be seen as not pulling their weight. So, while companies may be attracted to hiring extroverts because they interview well, bosses should remember to check their expectations—a gregarious personality doesn't necessarily equal better results.

Also, in the work place, introverts are often the calm in the center of the storm. When everyone is losing their head over the company's latest policy change—huddling in outraged groups in the break room or spouting off their impassioned opinions in meetings—introverts are already thinking of new ways to adjust. Quietly.

Finally, introverts really know their stuff. An introverted writer friend of mine is basically a walking encyclopedia of Celtic mythology. For example, if you ask him about the hero Cú Chulainn, he can not only tell you how he died but also what kind of chariot he drove around in. Listening to him talk, I've found myself thinking, "Wow, he really knows his stuff!" That's because introverts love learning and adding to their vast stores of specialty knowledge. It's no surprise that introverts often become experts in their field.

Introverts and Job Happiness, by the Numbers

As I researched careers for introverts, I started to wonder: What makes introverts happy on the job? What makes them unhappy? Are there certain jobs that introverts default to? To find out, I once again surveyed people who self-identified as introverts (readers of *Introvert, Dear*). Four hundred and six people responded. First, I asked them to rank how happy they were with their job on a scale of 1 to 5. Then I asked, "What is your job?" Jobs ranged from everything—from a teacher to an aerospace engineer to a vegan baker. One person wrote that they worked at a worm and cricket farm; their job was to raise giant mealworms. (Shout-out to you, Worm Master!)

You might imagine that the introverts who were happy with their jobs would report that they are librarians, writers, or truck drivers who spend a lot of time alone (typical "introverted" positions). But that wasn't the case. There was no clear trend about which jobs made introverts happy. Surprisingly, many introverts who were happy with their jobs had positions that were people-centric, such as being a psychotherapist, nurse, teacher, home health-care worker, manager, etc. In fact, roughly half had jobs that were typical "introvert" jobs, like accountant, bookkeeper, or writer; the other half had jobs that involved a lot of direct interaction with other people. These are introverts who reported that their job was "pretty great" or "amazing—it couldn't be better" (a 4 or 5 on the happiness scale).

I also asked introverts *why* they liked or disliked their job. Though I received a wide variety of answers, certain trends emerged. People who were happy with their job often said they liked it for the following reasons:

- I enjoy getting to help people and having the chance to make a difference in people's lives.
- There is just the right amount of people interaction—not too much or too little.
- I am often left alone, which allows me to concentrate for long periods of time.
- My boss respects me and does not micromanage me.
- My job gives me autonomy and flexibility.
- I get to be creative.
- I frequently get to learn new things.
- I love the people I work with.

- My company values its employees.
- I deal with clients mostly through email—not many face-to-face interactions.
- I have the option to work from home.

What about the introverts who were unhappy with their jobs? Again, there was no clear overall trend as far as what type of career they had. In fact, some of the same jobs that made the "happy" list also made the "unhappy" list, such as teacher, writer, manager, IT consultant, librarian, etc. That's right—there is an introvert out there somewhere who is surrounded by books and who is not happy! This person said they dislike their job because they have to share an office with someone, they don't get to be creative, and they don't have much control over their time. Did that just kill one of your introvert job fantasies?

However, there were some jobs that were clear losers. These jobs only appeared on the "unhappy" list, and respondents said these positions made them "miserable" or "not very happy" (a 1 or a 2 on the happiness scale). They were:

- Retail employee
- Call center agent
- Customer service representative

I suspect these jobs make introverts miserable because they have to interact with people frequently, and not in a meaningful way. "I have to act happy all the time," an introvert who works in retail writes. "I have to talk on the phone and be nice even when the other person is being abusive," a call center agent writes. "I have to deal with people who don't care about you, or others, for that matter," another retail worker laments.

Other reasons introverts disliked their jobs, whether they worked in retail, customer service, or something else, included:

- My job is boring and repetitive.
- It doesn't pay well.
- I am stressed and overworked.
- I don't get enough freedom and autonomy.
- There is a lot of turnover in the office.
- There is a poisonous work culture and too much office drama.
- My boss micromanages me.
- It's not my passion.
- I don't get enough time off.
- I have to make too many phone calls.
- I constantly have to meet new people and push myself out of my comfort zone.

My research isn't meant to be a comprehensive career guide, but I think it provides some important takeaways for introverts. The first is that introverts don't necessarily have to seek a solitary job. Some of the happiest introverts had jobs that put them in direct contact with people every day. Just make sure your job allows you to interact with people in a *meaningful* way. Troubleshooting angry customers' billing questions in a call center or telling people about the latest sale in a fake happy voice probably won't count as meaningful. It seemed like introverts who reported being happy with their jobs had stumbled into a type of Goldilocks scenario. You know, this porridge is too hot, this one is too cold, but, oh, this one is just right! These introverts spend part of their work day interacting with people and part of the day alone. They can close their office door when they need some quiet or occasionally work from home. In other words, they have balance. They don't have to be "on" all the time (only some of the time). They can retreat before an introvert hangover threatens.

Also, when considering a position, think about more than how much it pays and what your main duties are. Do you think you'll like and get along with your coworkers? Does your boss seem like the control-freak type who will micromanage you? To get a sense of the company culture and what your coworkers are like, try to meet some of them during the interview process. Have a short conversation with them. What kind of feeling do you get from talking to them? Do you seem to "click" with them? Will your introverted work style jive with theirs? Also, ask questions during the interview about how much you'll be expected to work in groups and collaborate. You may even go so far as to ask about the "personality" of the organization. Do people make a lot of chitchat during the work day and socialize outside of work frequently? Or do people mostly keep to themselves?

Perhaps most important, during the interview, make sure to ask how often you'll be expected to talk on the phone. Talking on the phone frequently was hands down the biggest complaint from introverts who disliked their job. If the job requires you to constantly make phone calls to people you don't know well, it's probably not for you.

When a Job Constantly Exhausts You

Colleen Sweeney is an introvert who ended up in a job that wasn't right for her—she worked for a major housewares retailer during the busy holiday season. "I knew from the moment I completed the first interview that this job was not going to be an enjoyable experience, based on the personality of the interviewing manager," she writes in an *Introvert, Dear* article. "She was what I would call a stereotypical extrovert: extremely outgoing, never took no for an answer, and just really did not understand introverts. As I got to know the other managers over the following weeks, I came to realize that my personality and theirs would not mesh."

Working in retail meant she was required to push the store's credit card on every customer, and "to not stop until they basically became belligerent toward us." As an introvert, she had a hard time doing this. She hated having to push people to do things that she herself would not like having pushed on her. And it was hard to deal with the constant rejection from customers. But she would do it again and again, all day long, because she and the other employees were being watched by their boss on camera. She would usually take a single "no" for an answer and move on. Her boss eventually noticed that her credit card sales record was almost nonexistent, and that led to another uncomfortable conversation for Colleen.

The most anxiety-filled moment came when she had to walk around the store trying to sell gift cards to customers. "I had to carry five on my person, along with some mints, and ask customers who appeared to be stuck on gift ideas if they wanted to purchase gift cards," she writes. "We also had to do this when ringing up customers, but it was much easier doing it there than randomly walking up to strangers. I knew that several managers were on the floor, and no doubt monitoring my every move. I did approach a few people, but was unsuccessful. At some point, my manager walked up to me and asked me how my sales were going. I did not lie; I told her the truth. At this point, she scolded me like a small child and insinuated that my job was on the line."

Colleen broke down in tears in the break room that day. It wasn't because she was afraid of losing her job—she had already decided she was not going to accept their offer if they asked her to stay on after the holidays. It was because she was so *uncomfortable* in her job, she writes. She ended up leaving the job one week before her trial period was up. "I honestly cannot say I regret leaving, because my mental health immediately improved upon giving my notice," she writes.

Today, she's moved on to a different job. But she still wishes some things in the retail industry would change. "The retail industry does not really care if a person is introverted," she writes. "They just want a person to make sales, and they do not really care if it makes a person uncomfortable." She understands that making sales is an important part of retail, but there are some things the industry could do to make this easier for everyone. For one, stores could create volunteer lists for employees to take on the "undesirable" jobs, like walking the sales floor selling gift cards to customers. Also, they could take an employee's personality into question when assigning them tasks. "The managers I had before the housewares store knew I was not comfortable working in the fitting room, so they took me off the roster for that zone," she writes. "I am not saying to give employees preferential treatment, but to realize they are not working to their full potential if they are not comfortable."

"I would love for introverts to be seen as completely 'normal' people, and not be considered weird because they are quieter and sometimes do not want to socialize," she adds. "I was ostracized because really rude customers deeply affected me, and because I was quiet."

Choosing the Right Field

So how do you choose a college major or career path that's right for you? To answer that question, I turned to Nancy Ancowitz, presentation and career coach, and author of *Self-Promotion for Introverts*. First, Ancowitz tells me in an interview, do some self-reflection and think about what helps you thrive. "Chances are, as an introvert, you prefer plenty of quiet time for activities like research, thinking, writing, and analyzing data, as opposed to back-to-back large group meetings," she says.

Then, think about what type of role you'd like to play in an organization. Would you prefer being an individual contributor, a team member, or a people manager—or any combination of these positions? For example, an individual contributor might be a freelance writer, a team member might take the form of being a social media strategist, and a people manager might be a project manager or the manager of a retail store. "Through self-reflection, paying attention to which activities give you energy and which drain you, you will discover what brings out the best in you," Ancowitz says. And if you're a student who has limited job experience, reflect on your experiences in school or volunteer work as starting points.

Most important, consider which rewards fuel you. Do you like getting accolades from managers and clients? Money? Intellectual satisfaction? Do you like learning new skills, helping others, or making a contribution to a cause? Even if your position or work environment aren't ideal, if you have the right motivation, you may find yourself gaining the emotional energy you need to keep going.

Finally, go on plenty of informational interviews to learn from pros in the fields you're interested in. If possible, job shadow. This way you can find out what a day in their work life is like before you commit. You may be surprised to discover how much a librarian has to interact with others or how much a journalist has to talk on the phone.

Ten Best Jobs for Introverts, Ranked by Salary

Tony Lee, publisher of CareerCast.com, has been writing about careers since the 1980s. Every year, he puts together lists of the best and worst jobs. Collaborating with two academics, in 2014, he compiled a list of ten jobs for introverts and shy people (Lee lumped shy individuals in with introverts because he figured they both wanted jobs that allowed them to avoid an overload of interactions with people each day). Lee and his colleagues thought about jobs that would play to introverts' strengths, as well as allow them to work quietly and independently at times.

Here is Lee's list, ranked in order of salary. All salary information comes from the US Bureau of Labor Statistics, according to Lee. "Projected growth" is how much this job field is expected to grow by the year 2020.

1. Astronomer—salary: $96,460/projected growth: 10 percent
2. Geoscientist—salary: $90,890/projected growth: 16 percent
3. Social Media Manager—salary: $54,170/projected growth: 12 percent
4. Film/video editor—salary: $51,300/projected growth: 3 percent
5. Court Reporter—salary: $48,160/projected growth: 10 percent
6. Archivist—salary: $47,340/projected growth: 11 percent
7. Industrial Machine Repairer—salary: $46,920/projected growth: 17 percent
8. Financial Clerk—salary: $36,850/projected growth: 11 percent
9. Medical Records Technician—salary: $34,160/projected growth: 22 percent
10. Animal Care and Service Workers—salary: $19,970 (caretakers); $25,270 (trainers)/projected growth: 15 percent

Work at Home in Your Pajamas (Really)

Making a living doesn't necessarily mean you have to hold down a nine-to-five job. Many introverts go the self-employed route, and this makes sense: we tend to be self-starters, we are independent, and we have big ideas. Furthermore, when you control how you work, you'll probably feel less drained at the end of the day. You're left with some energy and maybe even eagerness to socialize with your friends and loved ones. Here are some self-employment ideas for introverts:

- Graphic designer or web designer
- Coder
- Social media consultant
- Writer, author, copy writer, technical writer, or blogger
- Resume writer
- Photographer
- Private music lessons instructor
- Business or life coach
- Online tutor

The Introvert's Need for Meaningful Work

Are you like me? You know that career advice is helpful, but reading about salaries, projected job growth, etc., can leave you feeling like something is missing. That's because many introverts don't just want a paycheck—they want a calling, too.

They crave work that allows them to express their authentic selves—a career that embodies their interests, values, skills, and personality. In other words, they want to "do what they are." Really, in all areas of life, introverts don't feel "whole" unless their outer life reflects their inner life. If people can't see them for who they really are—the secret world inside them—they are inclined to feel fragmented and discontent.

It also comes down to a matter of time and energy. You likely spend a lot of time at your job: if you work full-time, you spend about 50 percent of your total waking hours on a work day "on the clock." You probably spend more time at your job on a work day than you do with your loved ones, alone, or doing meaningful hobbies (e.g., working on your novel). If you're going to clock this many hours doing something—and put in this much energy—you want it to matter. Introverts tend to have a small circle of close friends, because when we invest our time and limited energy into something, we want it to be exceptionally good; it's the same with our nine-to-five efforts.

As an introvert, finding a meaningful career is likely intertwined with finding yourself. You may feel like you can't build a career that reflects your identity until you figure out what that identity is. The downside is it can take a long time to discover who you really are—years or decades. And you may feel like you can't take action until you have complete information (introverts like to look before they leap). In the meantime, you may feel forced to settle for a day job to pay the bills. You hope to one day uncover your true self and, with it, your true calling. Unfortunately, settling for a day job is rarely satisfying. It may seem like your true talents and skills are being wasted on menial tasks. You feel meant for so much more.

Likewise, introverts approach their careers differently than extroverts. When searching for direction for their lives, extroverts tend to look outside themselves. They may ask themselves, *What careers are "hot" right now? How do my talents and skills fit with the existing landscape? What types of positions will earn me a good salary?* Introverts, on the other hand, tend to turn inward for direction. We do what feels authentic to us; we're guided by our own inner compass, not the winds of the world. This means we may not consider what will bring us more money, a higher status, another car, and a bigger house. Remember, introverts are less motivated by rewards than extroverts—this applies to our careers, too.

Often, introverts want their work to speak for itself. This is especially true when we're creating something, such as writing a book, building a business, or making art. We may feel uncomfortable monetizing our creations; we make art or publish the blog post because we care deeply about the expression itself. Likewise, we may shrink from marketing our products or services, because we loathe being the center of attention. We also want our work to speak for itself in the office or classroom. We rarely toot our own horn and shout, "Look at me!" We simply want to solve our client's problem thoroughly (and quietly). We want to earn an A on the paper, even if no one except the teacher sees the quality of our work.

When You Find Your Calling

As an introvert, it may not be easy to find your calling—but it can be done. Ann is an introvert who is a special education teacher. She's been teaching in some capacity for close to forty years. And she believes she's found her calling. "I love my students!" she tells me. "I love the challenge of finding how to support them in their learning." As an introvert, one strength she brings to the job is the ability to dive deep. "I will go online, or to the library, or to a bookstore to find what I need," she says. Being a special education teacher is different than being a classroom teacher, because she doesn't have to manage as many students. "I get to target individuals or small groups, which is where I feel I am most effective."

The days can get long. She can handle being "on" during the school day, but when she has to stay back after school for meetings, that's when she feels it and needs quiet. "When I get home there is *no* extra noise—not radio, not TV, not the computer," she says. "Some days it can get exhausting, so I need to allow time on the weekend to recover, too. If I need to stop for groceries or another errand on the way home, I avoid large stores—too much sensory overload!"

Even though the job can be tiring, Ann says there's nothing she'd rather do. "It is a stimulating job," she says. "I've been working in special education since 2001 and have not looked back."

Her advice to fellow introverts looking for their calling? Don't be afraid to change jobs if your current one isn't meeting your needs. Also, use personality assessments and/or career inventories to help you identify your strengths. "Sometimes you can access a community college to take a preference inventory," she says. "I did one in high school, and again after I had been in education for a few years. I went back to school at a time when my peers were starting to think about how many years they had until an early retirement. I earned two special education licenses then. Three years after that I tried graduate school, and a few years after that, I added two more licenses. Right now, I'm licensed in five areas. You can be shy or quiet, but you can still work towards your calling."

Tina is the founder of a community for music-lovers called The Daily Listening. She identifies her job as her calling because it is pretty much what she saw herself doing when she was a kid. "While I had no idea about the role technology would play back then, I knew that I loved music and that I wanted to be closer to it," she tells me. "The fact that I've built my career from the ground up really inspires me whenever I look back. I still have a long way to go, but just the notion of working towards a goal that I created on my own is my favorite part."

There are a lot of things she loves about her job. Probably the best thing is that she gets to work from home. "I don't have to worry about taking NYC's very crowded public transportation in the morning," she says. She also loves that she gets to combine her love for music with writing. Plus, there's that whole "making your own rules and controlling your own schedule" thing. As an introvert, flexibility is important to her.

Her advice to fellow introverts looking for their calling is straightforward: "Think about what makes you come alive, and go follow it."

Six Questions to Ask Yourself to Help You Find Your Calling

Still trying to figure out what your life's calling might be? Here are six questions you can ask yourself that can help point you in the right direction:

1. **What message do you want to share with the world?** Each of us has been shaped by a lifetime of experiences—and each of us has a unique message to share with the world. After learning about my introversion, my message became, "It's okay to be an introvert." If you could rent a billboard in Times Square for just one day, what would you put on it? In other words, what is the one thing you wish the world knew and understood?

2. **How do you want to be remembered when you're gone?** No one likes to think about what will happen after they die, but looking at the bigger picture can help you put things in perspective. Let's say you lived a full, rich life, and you are now ready to leave something behind for the ones you love—and for society. What would that legacy be? What qualities, ideas, or philosophies would you want others to have when you're gone? In what small (or big) way would you make the world a better place for others for years (or decades) to come?

3. **What did you want to be when you grew up?** What captured your imagination as a child? What careers fascinated you? How did you picture yourself when you daydreamed

about your life as an adult? Many of our aspirations were born in childhood.

4. **What kinds of tasks don't feel like work to you?** Think about your current job (or your experiences as a student, if you're still in school). There are probably some tasks you do each day that feel like utter drudgery, but there are probably other tasks that don't feel like work at all. These tasks are a cakewalk to complete, and you get compliments from others about them. Build your calling around these energizing tasks.

5. **What kind of work would you never do again, no matter how much you were paid?** Figuring out what is definitely *not* your calling can help you narrow your options. What kind of work can you just not stand?

6. **Who is doing your dream job, and what can you learn from them?** Think about the people in your life. Who has a career that you envy? Don't limit yourself to just the people you know—is there a "famous" person you have read or heard about who is doing a job you wish you had? Learn from them and the path they took. Do you need a license or a degree to do that job? More skills, or certain contacts in the field? Figure out how they got to where they are today.

In Closing

I've had a lot of jobs in my life. My first job was keeping the showroom clean in a furniture store. I had to dust, vacuum, and, worst of all, clean the toilets. Since then, I've worked as a tutor, journalist, editor, marketing assistant, teacher, and now author/publisher. During some of my worst jobs, I went to bed thinking, "Do I have to get up and do this all over again tomorrow?" When you have a job that makes you miserable, it becomes a slow-acting poison. It hurts not only in the moment but also well after the fact—because we introverts tend to think and ruminate so much. Jobs that sucked my energy left me with little desire to socialize or do my cherished introvert hobbies like reading and writing. I was just too drained.

The best job advice I can give you is this: go where you're celebrated, not just tolerated. Does your job make use of your introvert talents? Do you get to do things that play to what you truly excel at? Do your coworkers and supervisors see value in you? Most important, do you feel proud of your work? There is no perfect job out there, and you'll always have to make trade-offs, whatever you do. But if your job leaves you continually exhausted, perhaps it's time to make a change. It's never too late to make positive changes in your life. You might just find that a different job makes other parts of your life better, too.

Chapter 11

TROUBLESHOOTING YOUR JOB

It was rent day again, and her office was short-staffed. This has happened before to J. Lee Hazlett (the same J. who took on too many obligations in school). But it never gets any easier. "There are always too many residents, too many phone calls, too many questions," she writes in an *Introvert, Dear* article. "Even on a good rent day, when I have two leasing agents to handle the crowds and my personal attention is rarely required, I go home drained. Rent day is too much, too fast, and too loud."

On rent day, all of the residents of her apartment building seem to come in at once to pay their rent. Some want to chat as J. processes their payment. "When they're making small talk in bright, oblivious voices, it's a struggle to keep my desperate pleas to myself," she writes. "I ache for them to enter their PIN, take their receipt, and move along." Others pass her handwritten lists of maintenance problems they've been having for two or three weeks. "I'm torn between understanding and annoyance," she writes. "I now have a stack of new work orders to type. I watch helplessly as each successive request that comes across the counter whittles away a few more of the precious moments I might otherwise have had to recharge." To make matters even worse, the only other employee in the office on this particular rent day is new. She has lots of questions, and J. has to reply to them all. "And she can't wait, either, because Mrs. So-and-So from unit 4015 is tapping her impossibly long fingernails on my counter and sending her infamous sneer at both of us."

The tasks keep piling up on her desk, the phone rings almost nonstop, and people keep coming in the door. Keeping a fake smile glued to her face is draining. "What I want is to be left the hell alone for an hour, or two, or twenty. Maybe after that I'll be able—not ready, but able—to deal with more small talk and work requests." Pretty soon her smile becomes little more than bared teeth. She can hardly wait for her lunch break. "I watch the clock like an antsy schoolchild waiting for recess. In twenty minutes, fifteen, ten, it will be my turn to run away. But I don't want to use my outside voice and swing from the monkey bars; I want to curl up with my book and my meal and pretend that everything else has blinked out of existence. I want sixty minutes in heaven."

Despite what it seems like, J. doesn't hate her job. There are actually some aspects of it that she likes. "I love seeing the numbers come together when I make my annual budget. The minutiae of lease legalese fascinate me. Sometimes I even like to sit down and talk with my employees during slow times. But on rent day, there are no slow times, and even if there were, I'd be too busy trying to catch my breath to savor them."

At the end of the day, her focus and patience are shredded. But she has to keep acting like she's happy to see the people striding cheerfully through the front door. "I can't take my emotional exhaustion out on them, not only because this is my job but also because they've done nothing to deserve my ire," she writes. "They don't, for the most part at least, understand why I struggle every rent day."

Five o'clock comes, and J. is finally free. "I want to fly home, but I don't have the energy. I trudge instead. When I make it to my couch, I sink backwards, letting it take me deep into its comforting corduroy embrace. Peace. Safety. Relief. It's as if I'm a phone that's been plugged in just before the 1 percent reading on the battery bar flickers into nothingness. A calm, quiet night will have to pass before I'm fully charged and able to face the world again. But at least the worst is over for another month."

Have you had days like this on your job? If so, read on. In this chapter, we'll explore and troubleshoot some of the problems introverts experience at work.

When Friday Night Can't Come Soon Enough

Despite all the strengths introverts bring to the workforce, being an introvert on the job can be tough. I asked introverts what challenges they face career-wise. Here are some of the problems they deal with:

Having to be "on" all day. Shawn says, "I work as a warehouse clerk in a local hospital and do a fair bit of walking around, making deliveries, etc. I'm forever meeting people in the hallway, and this might sound odd, but it can be exhausting having to make eye contact and acknowledge each and every one of them during the course of a day. Truth is I would much prefer to have a job where I'm by myself 85 percent of the time."

Having to play nice with coworkers. "I'm a bookkeeper in a school, and I have to smile and be sweet and sugarcoat everything I say. It's really awkward since I've been raised to be honest and straightforward," Jane tells me.

Getting lost in your own thoughts. "The problem is that I live in my head, thinking about creative projects all day, and I don't always remember to smile at people when I should," Shawn says.

Small talk, small talk, small talk. Raven says, "I'm a school bus driver for special needs children. As long as I'm with my kids, I'm okay. It's when I have to be around coworkers that my introversion surfaces. I love caring for those less fortunate. Other people wear me out though. So many words! About so little substance! And the petty politicking! Oh my gosh, it's crazy. Working with the disabled keeps me grounded in what's important. The things that most people obsess over bore me. Celebrity and fame, who cares about those people?"

Struggling to speak up. "I'm soft-spoken, and I don't like conflict. So, if the staff is discussing an issue, I may not give my input. I may not stand up for myself. I will take the 'higher road' and let people say what they want, and I won't react," Michelle says.

Having to work with others frequently. Sally says, "Being asked by my boss to work in a group is hard. My mind goes blank, I get anxious, and it always turns out that, in a group, I contribute much less than if I do it alone. I feel stupid and awkward; but when working by myself, I shine! I can get more done by myself than working in a group!"

Constantly having to update other people on your work, instead of actually working. "I hate speaking in groups. I know my material but I hate weekly meetings. I do my work. I hate updating other people on what I am working on. Anything you need from me can be found in an email I've sent you," Robert says.

Having to approach strangers to sell something. "I worked for an advertising newsletter that required cold calling. I dreaded going to work every day. The only reason I didn't quit right away was because the pay was good. I quit when I moved to a new city and it was like I was a free woman!" Sally tells me.

Having to promote yourself. Melissa says, "You think your good work will get recognized, but management is easily fooled by some extroverts who know how to schmooze and appear to outperform others when they don't. Introverts don't walk around tooting our own horn."

Those distracting open offices. Adrian, who works in an open office, says, "There are too many people around. They are very loud and not focused on work a lot of the time. There isn't a place I can have some quiet time." Adrian's company uses a method called "hot desking," which is when there are more employees than desks, which supposedly forces employees to mingle and form new relationships. This sounds like an introvert's nightmare. Thankfully Adrian is the exception to the rule, because he always has the same desk, and no one else uses it. Still, he says, "I found myself more productive when in a small office, even with extroverts. When I can focus on a task, I am happier, but there is often too much noise and a lack of focus in the open office."

The expectation that you'll become buddies with your coworkers. "It's difficult that I am expected to bond with my teammates at work. Not that I don't like them, but I enjoy being alone most of the time. Sometimes I take my lunch earlier than others so I can have a happy lunch," Alyzza says.

Your coworkers think you're unsociable when you grab a few minutes to yourself. Bethani says, "I teach second grade. Sometimes during my planning time I turn the lights off and shut the door. My team (the other second grade teachers) has complained about it before. They think I'm being antisocial."

Having to fake being an extrovert. "I work in law enforcement so I'm forced to be extroverted and confrontational during certain situations. It was definitely out of my comfort zone, but I learned to adjust. Funny thing is I'm the complete opposite while off duty," Francisco says.

Constantly having to push yourself out of your comfort zone. Kristina says, "I'm in a super competitive field. It's hard to get in, hard to advance in further training, and the feedback I kept getting was to speak up more in group situations. Absolutely out of my nature and comfort level. But if I wanted in and wanted the advanced training, I needed to do so. I really, really wanted the job, so I did it!"

Social exhaustion. "I worked as a receptionist at a school a short while ago and found it really exhausting to be interacting with a huge amount of people in an eight-hour period," says Bryony.

Introverts and the Dreaded Interview

Perhaps one of the biggest struggles for introverts is the job interview. You can easily research job openings and think about how your skills might serve the company. You can write a grammatically correct and detailed resume and cover letter. But then the interview arrives, and your introvert skills seem to no longer serve you. Your introverted nature suddenly becomes your biggest liability.

It's one thing to just survive an interview. It's a whole other thing to actually sell yourself, impress the people bombarding you with questions, and shine. "The people who shine are most often the ones who feel energized in challenging social situations," writes Hayley Stanton in an *Introvert, Dear* article. "For introverts, it's overwhelming to be in a high-pressure situation like a job interview, being judged by strangers, when we attribute great importance to the outcome. When overstimulated, an introvert's mind might shut down to the extent that it can feel difficult to string a sentence together." Simply put, interviews don't bring out an introvert's best side.

Getting better at interviewing starts with becoming more comfortable with self-promotion, which is not something that comes naturally to many introverts. We may find self-promotion difficult because it forces us to talk about ourselves, when our natural preference is to keep our thoughts and feelings to ourselves. On the flip side, introverts may be comfortable promoting others because that doesn't involve sharing what feels personal or private. We're simply providing an opinion about something outside of ourselves.

To improve your self-promotion skills, start by thinking of them as just that—skills you can learn and practice. Just like learning how to speak a new language or how to play an instrument, you can get better at self-promotion. The first step is to think about what your strengths and accomplishments are. As an introvert, you might excel at making careful decisions, considering all angles of an issue, and doing conscientious work. Talk about those during the interview, and make sure to frame your introvert traits positively. Rather than saying, "I like to be left alone," try, "I do my best work when I am in an environment that allows me to have some time for quiet reflection."

Getting to know yourself includes thinking about the kind of environment you work best in. Although it's tempting to tell potential employers that you love working on teams and collaborating (because that's what you think they want to hear), be honest. Tell them that you will gladly pull your weight on a team, but as an introvert, you need some quiet time, too. Smart employers will appreciate your honesty.

Tobie Smith tried this "honesty is the best policy" approach in a recent interview. "Prior to being intentional about how I like to work, I gave the standard answer of, 'I really enjoy being part of a team,' and left it at that," she writes in an

Introvert, Dear article. "After giving some thought to how I prefer to work, I changed my answer to, 'I do my best work when I am in an environment that allows me to have some time for reflection.'" When she nervously used that answer for the first time in a panel interview, she was stunned by the results. "One of the panel members responded by not only commending me for giving such a thoughtful answer, but also by telling her fellow panel members that she could relate as a fellow introvert. Talk about a huge confidence booster!" Best of all, Tobie got the job.

Another way to get better at self-promoting is to not think about it as bragging. Instead, you're simply telling the facts. In your last position, did you streamline a process that saved the company time and money? Explain what you did and what the results were. And make sure to back up your claims with specifics. Instead of giving an opinion statement like, "I'm a strong writer," say, "I've been published in X publication, and I was very excited to be selected for the X award." It's not boasting if you're simply telling the details of what happened. Another tactic you can use is to take yourself out of the con-versation—quote someone else. Instead of saying, "I'm a strong web developer," try, "My previous manager told me that I'm one of the strongest developers at the company, and the CEO specifically requested that I be the lead developer on a project for an important client."

Finally, remember that if you don't promote yourself, no one else will! Other people talk themselves up all the time (especially extroverts). Why shouldn't you?

For Extroverts: What You Should Know about Interviewing an Introvert

Are you an extrovert who has been charged with interviewing job candidates? Although extroverts may shine in interviews, don't dismiss your quieter candidates. Here are four things you should know about interviewing an introvert, from Hayley Stanton's *Introvert, Dear* article:

1. **A panel interview is not the best way to assess our strengths.** As introverts, we do our best work inside our heads. When given time to reflect, we can thoughtfully present an idea in a way that others can easily grasp. Many of us can even be perfectionists, so it's unlikely you'll ever hear us say, "That'll do." Is that the kind of person you want to employ? Well, you might overlook that candidate based on their interview performance, especially if it's a panel interview. For introverts, it can be overwhelming to be in a high-pressure situation like a panel interview. If you must hold panel interviews, at least let candidates know who will be interviewing them beforehand, which will help them mentally prepare.

2. **We're not shy or rude. We're introverted.** When you first meet a candidate, you immediately make a number of assumptions about that person based on your own beliefs. This unconscious bias may lead to quick and inaccurate assessments. In the context of a job interview, many introverts struggle with making small talk. They

don't always come across as warm and friendly at their first meeting; sometimes it takes a while to get to know them. The first few minutes of meeting someone can be quite awkward and uncomfortable, and in these moments, the interviewer might assume that a quieter candidate is shy or rude. They may imagine how this could affect their ability to do the job, when in reality that person is actually introverted with traits that would be hugely beneficial in the role.

3. **We're reflectors, so we need time to think.** Many interviewers do not like long pauses after asking their questions. They want immediate answers. But that's not always possible for the thoughtful introvert. We process information deeply, and the rate at which information moves between areas of our brain is slower. We also rely more on long-term memory than working memory, which can mean it's difficult to access those "examples of a time when you . . ." When we do think of an example, quickly organizing our answer while feeling under scrutiny can be tricky—we're not all that good at thinking out loud. With that in mind, don't judge an introvert solely on their interview performance. Remember that awesome cover letter we wrote?

4. **It's time to rethink the job interview.** Employers, what qualities do you want in your next employee? For most roles, being a quick-thinker and fast-talker under pressure are not essential traits. However, isn't that

exactly what the traditional job interview is really testing? Think about what you could do differently during the interview. How could you give introverted candidates more opportunities to shine? Here are some ideas:

- Is it necessary to ambush candidates with questions they have never seen before? What if candidates were given the questions in advance? Email them the questions ahead of time, or at the very least, give them a handout when they arrive.
- Set a pre-interview task that gives candidates the opportunity to demonstrate their abilities. For example, if one of the job responsibilities is to write marketing copy for a catalog, have the candidate write a test blurb.
- Have a relaxed, one-on-one conversation with the candidate in addition to a panel interview.
- Give candidates the option to pass on a question and return to it later. This gives introverted candidates time to reflect.
- Always take the opportunity to look at a candidate's portfolio. There's no better way to assess their work.
- After the interview, encourage candidates to email you with additional thoughts.

"In one of the best interviews I've had, the lead interviewer explained the process and, to my surprise and utter delight, gave me the option to pass on a question if

I couldn't think of an answer right away," Hayley writes. She could return to that question at a later time. Throughout the interview, the interviewer asked thoughtful questions, drawing out better, more complete, answers from her.

"Afterwards, I had an honest one-on-one discussion with the interviewer," she writes. "He revealed that he feels nervous when interviewing. I explained that I'm introverted and reflective, and the need to be fast-thinking and quick-talking in a job interview means I don't shine so brightly." By honestly discussing their preferences, the two came to a mutual understanding—and in the end, Hayley got the job.

Talking Points to Sell Your Introvert Skills

Another problem introverts have in interviews is simply knowing what to say. For example, how do you describe your desire to work alone without coming across as unsociable? Here are four talking points to help you sell your introvert skills, from Katie McBeth's *Introvert, Dear* article:

"I'm the kind of team leader who makes sure everyone's voice is heard." The introvert's dislike of attention sometimes hinders us from receiving praise when it's due, or causes us to miss out on the stellar promotion that we deserve. However, when it comes to leadership skills, our desire to stay out of the spotlight can actually be a positive thing. It shows that we can work well in teams; our abilities to listen, absorb, and not micromanage a project or hog the stage can make us excellent team leaders. In other words, we make sure our voice isn't the only one being heard.

The takeaway: during your interview, bring up a time when you had to navigate around the needs of other team members. What role did you play in the team, and were you proud of your achievements, even if they went unnoticed by the majority? Focus on your love for doing a good job and being the supportive backbone of a business and your fellow employees. Talk about how much you want the business to succeed because of your hard work. Even if you're not in the spotlight, you're still playing a very important role.

"I can turn potentially negative situations into more positive ones." Emotional intelligence, also known as EQ, doesn't come easily for everyone. It's a mixture of intrapersonal intelligence and interpersonal intelligence. In other words, it's the ability to understand the emotions of others and the ability to control and manage your own emotions. When it comes to business, emotional intelligence is surprisingly powerful, so much so that it is now considered more important in hiring decisions than traditional IQ.

Luckily, empathic introverts are already well aware of their emotions and how to handle them. It comes easily for some of us, and we can use that to our advantage. Communication, management, and networking are all affected by EQ. Essentially, in any interaction in which another person's emotions may run high, your ability to navigate those difficult situations can be a tremendous strength to the business. The better the EQ, the more of an asset you will be.

The takeaway: Give the hiring manager an example of when you navigated a tough emotional situation with a former colleague or a customer. Showcase your empathy, and describe how it helped you turn a potentially negative situation into a more positive one.

"I believe in the company's mission." Company culture is a huge draw for introverts, and when you find a job that aligns with your values, it can be a winning ticket if you focus on the company's culture in the interview. Company culture is different for every business, but it's what creates a loyal employee base, a loyal consumer base, and a strong company that can withstand any issues that are thrown its way.

The takeaway: Since every business is different, it's important that you, the job seeker, study up on the company's message before applying to the job. If you find that their message matches what you're looking for, bring that up in the interview. Tell them you've been looking for a job just like this one.

"I'm in this for the long haul." Stability didn't always used to be such a huge benefit, but lately it can be the magic word for hiring managers. "You want to stay for a few years? Excellent!"

There's a good chance that you fall into the millennial generation. Millennials are the largest group to be entering the job market currently, and they are notorious for hopping from one job to the next every two years on average. However, introverts of any age have the competitive advantage of being fans of stability. When we search for a job, we're hoping this job will last a long time. Each of us has a different bandwidth for coping with change, but for introverts, usually the less large-scale change (such as switching jobs), the better.

The takeaway: Let the recruiter know that you're looking for stable and long-lasting employment. In our current state of the job market, with the constant turnover of younger employees, that is a rare trait to have.

Introverts Who Network (Yes, They Exist)

John is an introvert who regularly goes to networking events. How many he attends varies depending on his mood, schedule, and what events are available, but sometimes he goes to as many as five a week. And he's often there, looking chill in a suit and tie.

But it's not always easy to force himself to go. "My biggest challenges for networking come from getting motivated to just go out and talk," he tells me. "I've always considered myself to be a better listener than talker and found that oftentimes in networking settings it's difficult to utilize listening skills because there is so much going on." Another issue is dealing with the general anxiety of initiating conversations with strangers. "It really feels draining on me at times, but the more you go out and do it, the more natural it starts to feel."

John is a financial services representative who works in special needs financial assisting. Basically, this means he helps families who have kids with disabilities to plan for their financial future. The biggest benefit of networking, he says, is it reaffirms what he does, which is ultimately helping people. "The area I'm specializing in is fairly unique, and there aren't many people going around and talking about it, so if I'm not out there telling people it exists, then people aren't being informed or helped, which is really important to me," he says.

Katrina Razavi is also an introvert who has benefited from networking. A few years ago, she had a company. "Let me rephrase that," she writes in an *Introvert, Dear* article. "I had a domain name and an idea, but I had no money. In order to launch this 'company,' I had to raise money from investors. The problem was I didn't know anyone, and as a first-time entrepreneur, I didn't even realize what starting a company truly meant."

She quickly learned that she needed a solid professional network if she wanted to raise money, create partnerships, and meet other like-minded entrepreneurs. She embarked upon what ended up being a very scary, but life-changing journey—attending local networking events. "For an introvert, it was nerve-racking not knowing anyone *and* having to pitch myself and my business while gathering business cards," she writes. She almost always felt awkward and out of place. "For one, I was a young female at events usually filled with older, white males. Secondly, I couldn't shake the feeling of being an impostor. I constantly felt that my idea and company were worthless, and the only reason I got to where I was was through a stroke of luck."

Soon she realized that if she wanted this start-up to become real, she had to get better at networking. So she set out to improve her networking skills. She writes that most of it was trial and error, although she did read some books on how to improve her conversation skills, and she observed how "charismatic" people interacted. "It was scary and difficult, but after a few months, I got into the swing of it." Of course, Katrina is still an introvert.

"I'd much rather work alone with a cup of coffee than go to a social event with a ton of people I don't know," she writes.

Ultimately, Katrina was able to raise a hundred thousand dollars in capital for her business that eventually got acquired. "But the best thing to come out of that experience was the connections I made with people who were passionate about the same things I was passionate about," she writes. "The network I developed became my close friends, cheerleaders, and mentors. In fact, aside from the hundred thousand dollars we raised, a few years later when I looked for a job, someone in my network helped me get one with a twenty-thousand-dollar salary raise!"

Network without Changing Who You Are

Katrina learned a few things when she embarked on her journey to get better at networking, including, most important, the fact that she didn't have to change who she was to network. She could do it in her own introverted way. Here are some networking tips from Katrina:

1. **You don't have to be perfect.** Because introverts love to analyze, it's easy for us to fall into the trap of "I'm not great at socializing, so I'll just hold back what I have to say or how I feel." Instead of letting perfectionism get in your way, start off with small goals, such as making eye contact and smiling at someone. The reality is after you speak to someone, what they remember is how they *feel*. Often, they won't remember that you stuttered or that there was an awkward pause. They'll remember that you listened or cared about what they had to say.

2. **Use your introversion to your advantage.** One of the best strategies introverts can use is listening. Listening is a special quality of introversion that makes you more attentive and empathetic to have deeper conversations. That way you don't have the burden of having to "entertain" someone, and, therefore, you don't need to talk as much. People love talking about themselves. When you give someone the stage to talk first, specifically about themselves, you immediately establish rapport with that person. Asking leading questions is enough for you to continue a conversation. Here are some questions to help you with that:

   - Why did you feel that way?
   - How did you feel when that happened?
   - What happened next?
   - Tell me more about that.

3. **Build your "thriving environment."** Getting social doesn't have to mean huge crowds and approaching stranger after stranger. Introverts like smaller groups of people and one-on-one interactions, so tailor your social events accordingly. You could even try hosting your own mini-networking events. Introverts often like to play the host because it gives them more control over the event. About once every quarter, contact about ten people you roughly know. You could email, text, or even set up a Facebook event (no phone calls or face-to-face interactions needed). They may be coworkers, friends of friends, or acquaintances. Pick a date and invite them over to your place for wine and appetizers. Or if you don't want anyone in your home, choose a bar,

coffee shop, or restaurant to meet at. Only about five to eight will end up coming. Events like this beat the name tags and schmoozing. People are usually more relaxed, the group is smaller, and the connections are deeper. Everyone there is somehow "vetted" by you, so people feel at ease and are more open to interact.

Getting Noticed at Work without Turning into an Extrovert

In a perfect world your work would speak for itself—no self-promotion needed. Unfortunately, this isn't usually the case: you've probably seen in your own workplace that the employees who get promoted are doing more than just getting their work done. And, sadly, even the best bosses fall into the trap of playing favorites; the more they like an employee, the more competent they may consider that employee to be (even if it's not true).

This sounds like bad news for introverts. Playing the office politics game seems disingenuous, and frankly, it's not an area in which we naturally shine. But just like with networking, you don't have to turn yourself into an extrovert to get noticed—you can play to your introvert strengths. First, make sure you're building strong one-on-one connections. Everyone on your floor doesn't need to know who you are as long as a few key people (like your supervisors) know your name and like what you do. Introverts excel at making deep, lasting connections with others.

Also, look for little ways you can take initiative. If you're like me, you avoid the spotlight—which can result in being passive at work. Are there tasks that have been on your boss's to-do list for weeks? Or is there a problem that everyone on your team is ignoring? Take charge in your own quiet way and be the one to get it done. It doesn't have to be something major like volunteering to lead a committee. It could be as simple as noticing a problem and suggesting a solution to your boss. It could be even *simpler*, like being the one who changes the wall clocks to the correct time when it's daylight savings time (I've never known an office that didn't put off this annoying task). When you take initiative—even in small ways—your boss and coworkers will notice.

Along with taking initiative, take some time every day to make yourself visible. Extroverts get noticed because they're always in the break rooms and hallways, chatting and schmoozing. Introverts tend to stay tethered to their desks (we come to work, well, to *work*). You don't need to try to match an extrovert's high-energy efforts (this would be exhausting), but there are a few simple things you can do. For one, instead of heading straight for your cubicle or work station when you arrive, make a loop around the office and greet everyone. This could be as simple as smiling and saying two words: "Good morning." Or, make a point of replacing one email a day with a face-to-face conversation. Don't repeat it with the same person you talked to yesterday—choose someone different, so you get plenty of exposure. The best part of this strategy is it gives you a *reason* to talk to that person. Focus your conversation on the question they asked or the issue they raised in their email rather than making small talk. Words tend to flow more effortlessly for introverts when they're speaking to a task or impersonal objective rather than engaging in aimless getting-to-know-you chitchat.

Finally, become the go-to expert. Introverts love learning, so brush up on your organization's history, trends in your industry, your clients, company protocol, or whatever. If you're the person who always has the answer, you'll become indispensable to your employer.

How to Speak Up in Meetings When You're an Introvert Who Hates that Sort of Thing

When I worked in marketing, I often sat in on long meetings with VPs and other important figures. I found myself mentally poking holes in whatever plans they were making, yet I rarely spoke up, even if I had something valuable to say. I was just too intimidated; plus, I felt like I needed to form my ideas fully before I could open my mouth. I think many introverts fall into this trap. When you're an introvert, it can be hard to put yourself out there.

You may never become completely comfortable speaking up in meetings and having a roomful of eyes on you, but there are some things you can do to make it a little easier. For one, prepare for meetings ahead of time, even if no one asked you to. Gather your thoughts, look over your notes, and remind yourself of any key talking points you want to bring up. This extra preparation might give you the push you need to be one of the first people to speak up—even though that's probably not your style. In general, the sooner you can get your ideas out there, the better, because, on a psychological level, it helps you feel like part of the meeting earlier. Then, as the meeting goes on, people will tend to direct their comments to you, which helps you stay involved. This probably won't happen if you wait until later to speak up.

Also, let go of the idea that your thoughts have to be fully formulated before you speak. If you don't believe me on this one, sit back and observe your colleagues. You don't need me to tell you that people are always spouting off half-baked ideas—and no one seems to care. Half-baked ideas can have a lot of value; they serve as jumping off points that can move the group toward better ideas. Giving yourself permission to not be perfectly articulate may help you feel freer to express your ideas, "umms," "ahhs," and all.

When you do speak up, remember that it's okay to raise your voice and occasionally interrupt. One of the problems introverts often experience in group settings is we can't get a word in edgewise. We tend to be strong listeners and hate when others interrupt us before we've gotten all our thoughts out, so we wait until the other person is done speaking before we jump in. But the natural pause we're looking for may not come in a fast-moving group conversation. Try raising the decibel of your voice slightly more than the people around you. It shouldn't feel like you're shouting; instead, you're speaking in a voice that is slightly louder than what you normally feel comfortable using. This will get people's attention and signal that you're trying to jump into the discussion.

Finally, buy yourself time. If someone asks you a question and you don't have a snappy response, it's okay to say, "Why don't you come back to me because I want to think that through," or, "Can we table that idea for now? I want to think about it more." Jump back into the discussion when you have the answer. Or, because writing tends to be easier for introverts than speaking, send an email with your response later.

In Closing

By now, I hope you've internalized this secret: you don't have to transform yourself into an extrovert to succeed in life, or work. As an introvert, what works for you on the job is going to be different from what works for an extrovert—and that's okay. Give yourself permission to do things that play to your introvert strengths and needs. You can be dazzling in your own quiet way.

Chapter 12

INSIDE THE INTROVERT'S INNER WORLD

When I was a little girl, I was the star of a movie. The camera zoomed in for a close-up on my tears as I argued with my mom. It pulled back as I stared out my bedroom window at the stars, my mind filled with questions and snatches of thoughts. An ever-present narrator foreshadowed what was to come. As I walked into my classroom, the god-like voice said, "Suddenly, everything was different today." When I was riding my bike through my neighborhood at night, it warned, "She didn't know what was waiting for her in the shadows." My movie was full of beautiful, intimate moments, as well as drama, humor, and, frequently, suspense. In every scene, the actors' performances seemed authentic and raw.

But it was a movie no one would ever see. It all happened in my head. I was the director, producer, narrator, and star actor. There were no camera crews, makeup artists, or script writers. It was only me, and my vivid inner world.

Throughout my childhood, I often found myself drifting away to another world. (Sometimes I still do today.) This was a world where anything could happen. A young girl could get superpowers that allowed her to command animals. There was danger—or magic—always lurking just out of view. It was a world of probing questions and relentless curiosity. It wondered how my life was connected to other humans' lives forward and backward in time. My placid outward appearance belied how much was going on inside me. It was a secret only I knew. I had strong emotions and an inner monologue that rarely stopped, but I usually couldn't find the words to express the sum of what was on my mind.

What is it like in your inner world? In this chapter, we'll explore the introvert's mind. We'll tackle creativity, Resting Sad Face, overthinking, and more.

What the Introvert's Inner World Is Like

I asked introverts to describe their inner world. Here's what they told me:

It's an adventurous escape from reality. "My inner world changes, to be honest," Andrea tells me. "I'm always the centerpiece, but it's my escape from reality. I've gone on countless adventures. It's kind of like reading a book."

It's a place of comfort. "My inner world is a world of peace and harmony," Ghada says. "It is not wild and imaginative but homey and calm. It is a replica of my actual world yet with no clashes . . . a comfort zone."

It's a salvage yard. "I think my inner world is a little bit like a salvage yard," indie rocker jeremy messersmith tells me. "Any idea tossed my way gets examined and taken apart to see how it works. Sometimes ideas are rebuilt, sometimes they're scrapped or turned into pieces of art. It can be unrelenting sometimes, and it can be hard to switch off."

It's a continual search for truth and understanding. "My inner world is me searching through every dark alley and warned-about taboo. I'm looking for every hidden answer to the mystery of this so-called life, and in the end, all I've really learned is more about myself and less about everything I thought I knew," James says.

It's constantly analyzing the people around you. Ashley says, "I think about people and what makes them tick. I love investigating humanity. Some of my favorite things to think about are how alike we all are, despite our social status, where we may live, or what culture we identify with."

It's a movie with multiple alternative endings. "I'm playing out numerous scenarios that happened slightly differently, never happened, or could happen but likely won't. I often have to calm myself down from some intense emotion I sparked through whatever my imagination conjured. And often, I have very little control over outcomes unless I go all *Kill Bill* with it," Nicole says.

It pulls you in opposite directions. "For me, it's like there are two people arguing on issues all the time," Bishrul says.

It drives your creativity. "My imaginative nature gets transferred into creative action," Kelly says. "A desire to remodel my kitchen turned into hours of drafting and building new cabinet banks, Shaker doors, and intricate pullouts for garbage, recycling, pots and pans, etc. A desire to fill an empty wall space with artwork resulted in fixating on a gorgeous Thailand mountain line and turned into hours of learning the Bob Ross landscape painting technique to make my own masterpiece."

It houses emotions no one else sees. "My emotions play out on the canvas of my inner world," Brandon says. "I naturally tend not to express them too wildly in an outward sense, but they are rich and vivid on the inside. I've spent decades learning their nuances, to the point where I can often notice the second an emotion begins to bud and watch it unfold throughout my body."

It's an ever-changing landscape. "My mind is constantly writing stories and asking 'What if?' questions," Marissa says. "Whether it's plotting out the next scene in my fiction book, inserting myself into the Star Wars universe, or mulling over what I should have done differently in a real-world situation, I'm looking for patterns and plotlines that fit together. And sometimes it feels like a trap as my mind spins down into hopeless scenarios and imagined worlds where my worst fears come true."

It's made of hunches and feelings that transcend words. "Some people describe their minds as organized boxes, but mine is more of a rushing body of water with emotions, memories, thoughts, and inspirations all blending together," Mike says. "Sometimes it can be easy to describe in words, like if I'm focused on a memory or thinking about what someone said. However, other times, it is much more abstract. I'll be filled with an emotion I can't quite describe, but it's present and powerful nonetheless. I often feel like I'm close to discovering something just out or reach, or else I have discovered it."

It's full of imaginary characters and scenarios. Jill, a writer, says, "It includes all of my imaginary friends (a.k.a. the characters) that end up in my books. They're so vivid and real that sometimes I react to what they 'say' and 'do' with a facial expression. I also imagine wild scenarios like meeting celebrity hunks, being on reality TV shows, and winning an Oscar."

It's the fountain of your confidence. Lauren says, "In my inner world, I am the gladiator."

It's truly another world. "My inner world is endlessly expansive. I usually retreat to the vision I have for myself someday, a cozy cottage surrounded by trees and woodland creatures. But I also sometimes escape into worlds that are not realistic. They are magical and beautiful. Other times I retreat into places I've been to before where I was really happy," Amelia says.

It can't be easily described. Jessica says, "My inner world is kind of complicated. I'm not good at expressing what it's like." Laura says, "I wish a typewriter could just spill out all of my inner thoughts!"

Introverts and Creativity, by the Numbers

Introverts spend a lot of time reflecting, analyzing, and day-dreaming. Does this make introverts creative? To find out, I once again surveyed people who self-identify as introverts. A whopping 809 introverts responded—more than for any other survey! (Does this mean introverts are drawn to the topic of creativity?) First, I simply asked, "Do you consider yourself to be a creative person?" The results:

Yes—81 percent

No—19 percent

Wow! About four out of five introverts described themselves as creative. Maybe all that time in our head really does pay off.

Next, I asked about the types of creative activities introverts like to do. I gave them several options and said they could pick more than one. They could also add their own. They responded:

61 percent write or journal

42 percent paint, draw, do graphic design, or sculpt

16 percent create music

61 percent like thinking of new ideas

29 percent opted for something else—everything from knitting, photography, and filmmaking to woodworking, acting, and writing software. If you can name it, introverts are doing it.

Next I asked, "Do you think your introversion helps make you a more creative person?" The results:

Yes—74 percent
No—4 percent
I don't know—23 percent

I found it fascinating how the majority of introverts agree that their quiet, reflective nature boosts their creativity.

Finally, of the people who answered "yes" to the previous question, I asked *why* they thought their introversion helped make them more creative. I received 391 responses. Here is a sampling of what they wrote:

"I have more time to reflect than someone who's going out all the time."

"The creative process requires a lot of alone time to think, to feel, to process everything, then to bring it all out into the creative works. No one understands this more than introverts."

"Being introverted means I am not distracted by other people. In general, I am not concerned with what everyone else is doing."

"I think creativity comes from within, and we are wired to look inside first."

"As an introvert, I have a hard time expressing my feelings and prefer to do so with art."

"I am able to be quiet and just take in the world, take in humanity and its essence, process it in the hundreds of ways that introverts do, and create something that speaks to the human in all of us."

"I make the world inside my head come to life through art."

What Introverts Bring to the Creative Process

The numbers show that, generally, introverts are creative folks. Does this mean introverts are more creative than extroverts? That's a tough question to answer. I know a lot of creative introverts, like Anna, who draws dinosaur comics, or Brandon, who started a podcast about dead ideas. I know creative extroverts, too, like Misha, who built a website where anyone can trade services sans currency, or Adrianne, who photographs bands. For every creative introvert I personally know, I can tick off an extrovert who is creative. I believe both introverts *and* extroverts can be creative. However, introverts may have an edge. According to studies by psychologists Mihaly Csikszentmihalyi and Gregory Feist, the most spectacularly creative people in a given field tend to be introverted. Although they've found a way to be "extroverted" enough to share ideas with others and advance their own projects, they still see themselves as individuals who run separate from the herd.

Perhaps the greatest strength introverts bring to the creative process is our ability to work alone. And it's not just that we're *capable* of working alone—we *relish* working alone. Solitude has long been linked to creativity. Pablo Picasso believed that artists could never accomplish any serious creative endeavor unless they worked alone. Likewise, psychologists agree that solitude is essential to doing our best creative work. The distinguished psychologist Hans Eysenck once noted that introversion and creativity go hand-in-hand because working alone allows a person to better concentrate on the task before them; also, spending less time with other people conserves energy for creative work. Conversations with others may inspire us, having new experiences may spark ideas, and our relationships may connect us to the greater whole, but it's in solitude that we excavate the riches of our hidden inner world.

Perhaps unsurprisingly, Reed Larson, a professor of human development and family studies at the University of Illinois at Urbana-Champaign, found that adolescents tend to report feeling less self-conscious when they're alone. In the 1990s, he gave teenagers beepers and checked in with them randomly throughout the day, asking them to record what they were doing, who they were with, and how they were feeling. Reed found that the teenagers did not report feeling happy *in the moment* when they were by themselves; however, they did report feeling better *after* they had spent time alone. Also, he found that when alone (away from the gaze of their peers), teens felt less self-conscious. This state of mind is important to creative work because it frees us up to follow artistic impulses. You probably can't come up with original ideas or let your emotions out in an authentic, expressive way if your mind is distracted with worries about what others think of you.

Another key to creativity is the ability to let your mind wander. Researchers have a name for when you zone out, daydream, or let your mind drift from topic to topic; they call it "creative incubation." It means you're not consciously thinking about a problem, but your mind is still working on it in the background, like an app running on your smart phone even when you're not using it. Suddenly, while you're doing the dishes or taking a shower, an idea dawns on you—"aha!"—like a light bulb turning on. Who's great at turning inward, daydreaming, and letting their minds wander? Introverts.

Finally, introverts tend to be observers. We may not say much, but we notice a lot. How your friend's eyes flickered ever so slightly but guiltily when he swore he didn't intentionally forget to invite a mutual friend to his birthday party. The delicate way the sunlight casts shadows on the old stone wall. The crunchy reds, browns, and golds of fall leaves on the forest floor. All these observations tumble around in our minds and enrich our ideas.

Famous Creative Introverts

- Shonda Rhimes, creator of *Grey's Anatomy* and *Scandal*, who writes in her memoir that she's always been an introverted person who didn't go out to Hollywood parties
- David Letterman, long-time former host of the *Late Show*
- Harrison Ford, actor
- Gwyneth Paltrow, actress
- John Green, author of *The Fault in Our Stars*
- Elton John, musician
- Larry Page, co-founder of Google
- Emma Watson, actress
- Courtney Cox, actress, who calls herself a "homebody"
- Steven Spielberg, director and producer
- Felicia Day, actress, a self-professed introvert who writes in her memoir that she felt overwhelmed when she had to have people work for her
- Mark Zuckerberg, creator of Facebook

- Audrey Hepburn, actress, who was quoted as saying, "I'm an introvert . . . I love being by myself, love being outdoors, love taking a long walk with my dogs and looking at the trees, flowers, the sky"
- Meryl Streep, actress
- Dr. Seuss, author, who, according to Susan Cain, was afraid of meeting the children who read his books because he thought he would disappoint them with how quiet he was
- Frederic Chopin, composer, who only gave thirty public performances in his lifetime
- Lady Gaga, musician, who has said that she likes to keep to herself and focus on her music

Harnessing the Creative Power of Solitude

It's not just researchers and psychologists who believe that solitude is crucial to creativity. Famous artists, writers, and innovators agree. For one, J. K. Rowling, a self-professed introvert, credits her "shy" nature with helping her come up with Harry Potter. Maybe you've heard the story. She was riding on a train when suddenly the idea for the series popped into her head. (Sounds like "creative incubating" to me.) She was alone and didn't have a pen—but she was too shy to ask another passenger for one. Ultimately, she believes this was a good thing. Instead of trying to work out her ideas on paper, she simply sat back and thought for the length of the train ride—about four hours.

The details of a "scrawny, black-haired, bespectacled boy" who didn't know he was a wizard bubbled up in her brain. If she had stopped to capture the ideas on paper, she might have slowed them down and stifled the creative process completely, Rowling explains on her blog.

Ernest Hemingway, one of the great American twentieth-century novelists, also believed in the creative power of solitude. In his 1954 Nobel Prize acceptance speech, he said that when writers spend less time alone (i.e., are less "lonely"), the quality of their work declines. While organizations for writers give them opportunities to socialize, Hemingway doubted that they actually improved their writing.

Likewise, Steve Wozniak is also said to be an introvert. While working alone late at night, he invented the world's first user-friendly computer; he would later go on to co-found Apple with his extroverted counterpart, Steve Jobs. In his memoir, Wozniak writes that engineers and inventors are like artists, and, just like artists, they work best alone—not on a team, not in a corporate office, but alone.

Finally, there's jeremy messersmith. Creativity, for him, is "a lot of just sitting at the computer by myself." He tells me, "Art is a way for me as an introvert to dive into myself. It's self-exploration." He recently spent a whole summer writing songs alone in a gazebo. When he writes, he examines his personal experiences, sometimes diving into his childhood. And he believes his introversion helps make him more creative. "Creativity requires taking time for yourself and really examining and questioning yourself," he says. "I'm reminded of a quote by e. e. cummings I like a lot: 'The Artist is no other than he who unlearns what he has learned, in order to know himself.' I think introverts are uniquely equipped for that kind of inner voyage."

"Are You Okay?"—Resting Sad Face

People are always asking Lauren Zazzara, "What's wrong?" Her friends, her family, her coworkers—people who know her well—will ask her this question even when everything is perfectly fine. That's because Lauren has something she calls "Resting Sad Face." You've probably heard of its counterpart, "Resting Bitch Face," which is when someone looks mean or angry without intending to. Lauren, on the other hand, just looks unhappy.

"If I'm not up, it's assumed I'm down," she writes in an *Introvert, Dear* article. "Which makes me feel like it's not okay to be anything other than what others feel I should be."

Resting Sad (or Bitch) Face is often a by-product of mind-wandering or creative incubating. It can also happen when an introvert is doing nothing at all. For Lauren, it happens anytime she turns inward. It takes energy to act happy and excited when she's around other people. When she's not talking to someone, she returns to her inner introvert world. "I'm often told that I'm in my own world (which often results in me walking into things or other people, but that's a whole other can of worms)," she explains. This is when people start asking her what's wrong. She understands that it's out of concern, but it gets old.

"It's even more frustrating when I'm told to smile," she writes. "Thinking isn't really conducive to smiling, and in my opinion, it would be much stranger if I was pondering to myself with a huge grin on my face rather than my normal, concentrated look. Is it wrong for me to be just thinking? Why should I owe anyone a smile?"

This sort of thing happens to me all the time. But I would call my problem "Something's Wrong" Face. In fact, on two

ARE YOU OKAY? YOU LOOK UPSET...

THAT'S MY "THINKING" FACE!!

different occasions while writing this book, one of my very extroverted neighbors approached me when I was working in my apartment's common area. "Is everything okay?" he asked, interrupting my typing *and* my concentration. "You just have this look on your face like something bad is happening." I had to summon all my patience to answer in an even tone, "Everything's fine." How ironic that he asked me this while I was literally writing a book about understanding introverts better.

When you're in your inner world, what does your face look like? If you wear a sad or intense expression like Lauren and I do, welcome to the club.

The Torture of Overthinking

Unfortunately, on the other side of mind-wandering, creative incubating, and daydreaming is something far more sinister: overthinking. According to psychotherapist Amy Morin, author of *13 Things Mentally Strong People Don't Do*, overthinking usually involves two destructive thought patterns: ruminating and worrying. Ruminating is when you rehash the past ("I shouldn't have said that"), while worrying is when you make negative, often catastrophic, predictions about the future ("I'm going to embarrass myself on the date"). And often, overthinkers don't just think in words; they conjure up terrifying images to accompany their thoughts—a devastating car crash or a vicious argument with a significant other.

Overthinking can also cause your brain to play a memory over and over again, like a song stuck on repeat. *Did I really mess up as badly as I thought I did?* you think. *What did he really mean when he reacted like that?* Like a detective, you're trying to extract a key piece of information by going over the evidence again and again. Or you may imagine all the things you could have done differently. "I should have said *this*, not *that*" or "Why did I choose this college major? Or this job? Or this relationship?" Your brain becomes obsessed with past events you can't change.

Ashley told me that her overthinking stems from feeling self-conscious. "I think too much about other people's thoughts," she says. "It prevents me from doing what I want for fear of how others will respond." Christianne told me that she ruminates on things she could do or has done, even though she recognizes that this behavior is counterproductive. "It fuels my anxiety but doesn't fix anything," she says.

Other times, your imagination runs away with you. One moment you're enjoying something pleasant, like a walk with your significant other, and the next moment a dark thought enters your mind. Jill says her overthinking usually starts small then spirals almost comically out of control. "One minute I'm thinking, *This song has a good life message*, and the next minute I'm planning my funeral slide show after I died heroically fighting the terrorists at the mall."

What Overthinking Feels Like

Everyone overthinks sometimes, even extroverts, but introverts are probably more prone to it. We may not even notice when we're doing it because overthinking is like second nature to us—at least, that's what several introverts told me. I asked introverts, "When you notice you're doing it, what does over-thinking feel like?" and this is what they said:

"Overthinking feels like having a million tabs open at once."

—Tina

"Like a slap back to reality when you realize that you still have to have a difficult talk with someone after you have already had the conversation in your head, multiple times, in multiple different ways."

—Tiffany

"It's like a black hole that brings me deeper and deeper in. One choice spins me into a million possible outcomes or possibilities. I worry how my choices affect others or what will happen ten years from now."

—Julie

"It feels like a fog when I'm in it, so much so that sometimes I'll say something out loud from some made up scenario that had nothing to do with the present. It's embarrassing even when I'm alone."

—Nicole

"It feels like I'm incapacitated, and I can't make a decision. I'm adaptable and strategic, so the combination of all the possibilities that could happen keep coming to the point where I don't know what to do anymore. I tend to get anxious as a result. It's not just decisions, but what people mean when they say stuff tends to lead to that anxiety and overthinking when it really can be nothing."

—Hillary

"For me, it feels like your brain is at a busy intersection and all the traffic lights are blinking randomly. Truckloads of information zoom through without any sense of direction."

—Robert

How Overthinking Harms You

When you can't get out of your head, it can put you in a state of anguish and take a serious toll on your well-being. Research published in the *Journal of Abnormal Psychology* finds that dwelling on your shortcomings, mistakes, and problems increases your risk of mental health problems, such as anxiety and depression. And as your mental health declines, you tend to ruminate even *more*, leading to a nasty cycle that is difficult to break. Isabelle, a chronic overthinker, knows this all too well. "Overthinking causes me anxiety and depression, but it also makes me aloof and not very present," she tells me. "I can zoom out of a conversation because my brain decides to go on a journey, and then I miss bits and feel super guilty for being a lousy friend, sister, or partner, adding to the anxiety and depression. Honestly, nothing good has ever come from overthinking in my case."

Overthinking can also keep you from being productive. Sally, another chronic overthinker, tells me, "Overthinking leads to being overwhelmed, which leads to inaction." Likewise,

Marianne says, "When I overthink, it brings more stress, and I feel paralyzed and unmotivated." This results in a state of mind that can make it feel impossible to make decisions (even little ones), tackle your homework assignment, or check things off your mounting to-do list.

Worst of all, overthinking seems to strike at the most inconvenient times. Have you ever found yourself lying awake late at night, unable to sleep because you're playing a mistake from five years ago over and over in your head? There's absolutely nothing you can do about that situation now, but you can't get to sleep because your mind won't shut off. A study published in *Personality and Individual Differences* confirms this, showing that rumination and worry lead to poorer sleep quality and fewer hours of sleep. Overthinking is the worst.

How to Stop Overthinking

How do you break the rumination cycle? It's not easy, but with some effort, it can be done. Here are some ideas to help you break free of unproductive overthinking:

1. **Notice when you're overthinking.** Like I said, many introverts don't even notice when they're overthinking because it's so normal for them. The first step is to simply start being aware of when you're ruminating, and to recognize that this pattern of thinking is unproductive.

2. **Try to put things in perspective.** This is easier said than done. That awkward thing you said at work really does seem awful right now. But before you conclude that

your comment will get you fired, acknowledge that your thoughts may be exaggeratedly negative. In other words, you may be making a bigger deal out of the issue in your head than it really is. Train yourself to recognize and replace thinking errors before they work you into a wide-awake-at-two-in-the-morning frenzy of overthinking.

3. **Change the channel.** Do something that disrupts your train of thought. Get out of the house and take a walk—sunlight boosts the levels of a natural antidepressant found in the brain. Listen to music. Talk to someone, even if it's not about what's currently on your mind. Do anything to get your mind going down a different track.

4. **Breathe.** There's a reason why this advice is a common refrain of pop psychology—it really does reduce stress. The key is to breathe deeply from your abdomen, getting as much air as possible into your lungs. Try these techniques:

   - Sit comfortably with your back straight. Put one hand on your chest and the other on your stomach.
   - Breathe in through your nose. The hand on your stomach should rise. The hand on your chest should not move much.
   - Exhale through your mouth, pushing out as much air as you can. At the same time, contract your abdominal muscles. The hand on your stomach should move in as you exhale, but your other hand should not move much.
   - Keep breathing in through your nose and out through your mouth. Try to inhale enough so that your lower abdomen rises and falls. Count s-l-o-w-l-y as you exhale.

- Then, imagine yourself letting go of whatever is bothering you.

5. **Take action.** When we get wrapped up in overthinking, we may put off making decisions (I'm guilty of this). We're looking for the "perfect" or "right" answer. But life is messy, and rarely will you be able to make a decision that has zero trade-offs. Sometimes making *any* decision is better than being stuck in indecision, especially when it comes to "little" things like if you should go to the social event or not. For bigger questions—like what college to attend or if you should stay with your partner—take small steps to move yourself forward. Only focus on one step at a time. If your choice doesn't feel right, you have permission to change your mind.

In Closing

The little girl who saw her life as a movie also told stories to herself in her mind to help herself fall asleep at night. She wrote books on construction paper and entertained her cousins with games she made up. This girl grew up to be a teenager who daydreamed in class and wrote snatches of poetry in the margins of her math assignments. She stared out the window and thought big thoughts about the world. It eventually led her to write about topics she cared deeply about in an effort to help other people. I guess you could say I have always lived partly in this world and partly in the world of my mind. I believe I always will and, as an introvert, I suspect that you will, too. Where will your inner world take you?

Chapter 13

WORK WITH YOUR INTROVERSION RATHER THAN FIGHT AGAINST IT

When Dave Rendall was a child, he was always trying to make people laugh. Hyperactive and attention-loving, he was the typical class clown. "I was a bad kid—at least, that's what everyone told me," Dave writes in his book, *The Freak Factor*. "I was told repeatedly I was obnoxious and immature, had a bad attitude, and lacked self-control. Even my parents called me 'motormouth' because of my nonstop chatter." Because of comments like these, Dave didn't have a lot of hope for the future. "You can only hear people tell you something is wrong with you for so long before you begin to believe them," he writes.

His problems seemed to follow him almost everywhere he went. Only a few weeks into his job at a large nonprofit, his boss and a few colleagues sat him down. They had a lot of complaints about him. "I didn't ask for their input, and I talked too much, too often, and for too long in meetings," he writes. "I didn't seem open to their involvement." If Dave didn't make some major changes soon, his boss told him, he'd be out of a job.

Seeing the writing on the wall, Dave quit and took another position. But things weren't much better there. His work style clashed with his boss's. As a result, he was constantly frustrated and irritable. His weight began to balloon as his eating habits and sleep patterns deteriorated, and every day became a battle. Once again, Dave's boss gave him the "change your ways or else" talk. That's when it hit him—he needed a drastically different approach.

At that point, Dave could have gone down the traditional self-development route, which is to focus on fixing your weaknesses. Instead, he chose a different way. "I didn't improve by overcoming my weaknesses," he writes. "I didn't really change myself at all. I succeeded by *flaunting* my weaknesses and *finding situations* that valued the positive side of my apparent flaws."

Think about that for a moment. Instead of changing himself, he changed his situation.

Dave quit his job as a manager and started working as a college professor. This change allowed him to teach two of his favorite topics: strategy and managing change. He also started a business that helped companies with strategic planning. He found that his clients appreciated his strategic thinking and ability to help them see the big picture. Gradually he transitioned from consulting to training to professional speaking. Today, he's a successful speaker and author. He's spoken to audiences on every inhabited continent. He's given talks to the United States Air Force and the Australian government, as well as to numerous Fortune 500 companies, like AT&T, State Farm, Ralph Lauren, and GlaxoSmithKline. As a keynote speaker, he's often praised for his energy and enthusiasm. He believes his passion helps him connect with his audience.

Dave loves it. And he's gotten his health and sanity back. "I've lost weight and started running marathons, ultramarathons, and triathlons," he writes. "I feel energized and confident. My work provides me with happiness, fulfillment, and a sense that I have truly found my calling."

No one criticizes Dave for his weaknesses anymore. But don't get him wrong. He'll be the first to tell you that all his old flaws are still there. His flaws just don't matter anymore.

"What Makes You Weird Also Makes You Wonderful"

I've met Dave, and I can tell you that he's very much an extrovert. He's the kind of guy you can't miss. He's over six feet tall and loves wearing anything pink—pink shoes, pink suit coat, you name it. He has a lot of energy, and when he gets on stage to speak, people listen. You probably can't relate to some parts of his story (being overly talkative and attention-loving). Nevertheless, I wanted to share it with you. Like many introverts, Dave, too, had some aspects of his temperament that seemed to be less than ideal. Troublesome, even.

I share Dave's story because he did something that is counterintuitive for most people—and it worked. He didn't take the approach that is normally recommended for improving oneself. He didn't make a five-step plan to talk less. He didn't meditate on the mantra, "Calm down and stop talking, calm down and stop talking . . ." Instead of focusing on his weaknesses, he leaned into the things that he was already good at. Job-wise, he went where he was celebrated, not just tolerated.

There's a powerful lesson in Dave's story for all of us.

Don't get me wrong. There's immense value in improving your skills. Becoming a teacher forced me to become more comfortable with the spotlight. Going on dates helped me get better at the give-and-take of conversation. Likewise, Andre made a plan to improve his social skills (Chapter 2), Shawna decided to make more friends when she moved to a new city (Chapter 5), and Katrina worked on her networking abilities (Chapter 11). That's not the kind of self-improvement—improving some basic skills if they're lacking—that I'm talking about here.

Dave likes to say, "What makes us weird also makes us wonderful. What makes us weak also makes us strong." In other words, on the other side of your weaknesses are your strengths. This advice can apply to anyone, of any temperament or personality. But here, I'm going to apply it to introverts. So you're quiet and you don't always know what to say? On the other side of that "weakness" is a powerful, analytical mind. You get overstimulated more easily than others? In your solitude, you solve problems, think of new ideas, and create. You "umm" and "ahh" when you speak? Your reflective mind processes things deeply. Instead of seeing your introvert qualities as your biggest flaws, consider that they may actually be your biggest strengths.

Do keep on improving your skills and work on the things that hold you back. You can do it. But make sure you don't miss the big picture—seeking situations that play to your natural strengths. That's how you'll get ahead and build the kind of life you really want. Job-wise, find a career that demands that you use your introvert skills, whether it's social work, social media, leading a company, or building your own. When it comes to the close relationships in your life, surround yourself with only those who energize you, not drain you. Your good friends and significant other should leave you feeling richer and fuller after being around them. You have no obligation to maintain one-sided friendships or toxic relationships.

Introverts have a tendency to internalize things. When there's a problem in our lives, we turn inward and point the finger of blame squarely at ourselves. There's nothing wrong with taking responsibility for your actions; in fact, I believe the world would be a better place if everyone had a strong sense of personal responsibility. But many introverts go overboard in this area. When we find ourselves in a soul-sucking job or a draining relationship, the first thing some of us do is try to adapt *ourselves* to the situation. We bend to everyone else's needs and forget about our own. While being adaptable can be a good thing, being *too* adaptable can be downright dangerous. It means you start living inauthentically. It means you bend so much that you don't recognize yourself anymore. And this can lead to a life of perpetual exhaustion.

Change your situation, change your life.

Your Needs Are Just as Important as Everyone Else's Needs

As this book comes to a close, I'd like to leave you with three big ideas. The first one is this: Your needs are just as important as everyone else's.

A few years ago, Lauren Sapala worked for a small start-up. The company had a tight budget, so Lauren found herself crammed into a tiny office with ten other people. "The woman who sat next to me wore a strong perfume that reminded me of the candle store in the mall," she writes in an *Introvert, Dear* article. "Usually by mid-morning, I had the beginnings of a throbbing headache, and by the end of the afternoon, I was downright nauseous."

At this point in Lauren's life, she hadn't yet discovered that she is an introvert (as well as a highly sensitive person). "I just knew that I did not mix well with strong smells, loud noises, or crowded places. I was prone to headaches and anxiety, and something as simple as a strobe light could set me off." Even though this woman's perfume seemed like such a small thing, it was wreaking havoc on her daily life.

Lauren had become close with one of her coworkers who was very similar to Lauren—intuitive, people-oriented, and sensitive. The difference was her friend was an extrovert, and she had a different take on the perfume lady. When Lauren told her about it, she said simply, "Why don't you ask her not to wear that perfume to work anymore? Tell her it bothers you."

Lauren was stunned, and speechless. "That was *allowed*?" she writes. "I could ask other people to modify something because it was causing me a problem? Rationally, I understood this concept. But emotionally, it felt like my entire world had shifted."

When You Have to Speak Up

It's not uncommon for introverts—especially sensitive, intuitive introverts like Lauren who are very tuned into people—to not speak up for their own needs. When you're an introvert who notices *everything* about people—like their tone of voice, their body language, the look in their eyes, and the words they're *not* saying—you notice how they react to you, too. You notice when you're making them slightly uncomfortable. When you're inconveniencing them, even if they aren't saying so. If you're an introvert who has a high level of empathy (as many introverts do), you put yourself in their shoes. How would they feel if you told them to stop wearing that perfume? Because you think a lot about other people's feelings, you try to be as considerate as possible.

The problem with always putting other people first is that your needs can get overlooked. People may not even know they're doing it, because you're working hard not to show that you need something. You're hoping that somehow, intuitively, they'll just read your mind. As a sensitive introvert, you tend to pick up on little cues, so naturally you expect that others will, too. Sadly, this isn't usually the case. It's like what happened with Lauren. The perfume lady didn't even know she was causing a problem that was wrecking her day—again and again.

Lauren writes that speaking up for ourselves is hard because it brings up emotional baggage from the past. "Most of us have felt for our entire lives that our personal needs are weird and inconvenient to others," she writes. "We need more space than other people. We need more time. We need more complexity, and more depth. Because other people are often confused by these needs, or can even feel rejected in some way, we learn as children to compromise on them constantly. So, instead of figuring out how to negotiate with others for what we need, we withdraw further into our inner world, attempting to meet all of our needs there, totally on our own."

Some people seem to naturally stand up for their needs. This trait is apparent in the way they walk, talk, and even look at others. Bullies and emotionally needy people steer clear of them. Instead, they prey on another type of individual—the person whose gaze is at their shoes, who apologizes even when it's not their fault, and who works to keep the peace, no matter what need of theirs must be sacrificed.

When you stand up for your needs, you may get reactions from other people that aren't fun to deal with. But there's power in saying the truth. Although people might not like what you say, your honesty shows them something important: that you care enough about the relationship that you're willing to be vulnerable and real with them. You may find that when you speak up for your needs, people respect you more. It shows you value yourself and believe you're worthy of respect. When you see yourself as a person who is worthy of respect, others will, too.

If you're committed to living your best life, speaking up for your needs must be done. "The more you do it, the more you'll be able to readily identify what's yours, what belongs to other people, and how to draw the line between the two," says Lauren. "You'll come to a place where you step into your own power consistently, with passion and purpose. And when you look into the mirror, you'll respect the person looking back at you."

If you're an introvert who struggles to speak up, remember that your needs are just as important as everyone else's. You're a part of "everyone." You matter, too.

Live Fearlessly

When Susan Cain walked onto the TED stage in 2012 to give her now famous talk, "The Power of Introverts," she made the whole thing look easy. Carrying no notes, she opened with a story about summer camp and went on to perform a camp cheer. Then, before an audience of 1,500 people, she critiqued a society that favors the kind of person who craves an audience. Her talk was a smash hit—she received a standing ovation. And her message continues to resonate today; at the time of writing this book, her speech has almost sixteen million views online, according to TED.com.

But it wasn't easy. Even twenty-four hours before her talk, she was tweaking her speech and re-memorizing parts of it. Prior to that, she had joined Toastmasters, an organization whose members meet weekly to practice public speaking. Also, she had scheduled a two-hour crash course with TED's speaking coach, who gave her voice and breath exercises. As the date of her talk came closer, Susan suffered a few sleepless nights. She started to wonder if she'd rather *die* than give this talk.

I made the mistake of asking Susan if she was nervous when the day of her talk arrived. "Was I nervous? Was I nervous?" she responded. "Oh yes. I was in a full-on state of panic." She tells me she "literally couldn't have done it" without the week of prep she did beforehand with a very emotionally sensitive and attuned acting coach, Jim Fyfe. "And I also couldn't have done it if I had felt that there was any other alternative. But who's going to say no to giving a TED talk about a subject she's so passionate about—that she's just devoted the last seven years of her life to writing a book about? So really, there was no choice," she says. "I had to do it!" And then, almost miraculously, in the months and years following the TED talk, her fear of public speaking mostly dissolved. "I say mostly because it's still a bit uncomfortable—but within a totally manageable zone," she tells me.

How did she transform herself into someone who no longer panics about public speaking? "The key is that you have to expose yourself to the thing you fear in small, manageable chunks," she advises. "Do not start your public speaking career with a TED talk! Start it by standing up in front of your two best friends and telling them what you had for dinner. You can ratchet it up from there. It really is possible! I know this because I was the person who, ten years ago, would have told you that it wasn't."

Musician jeremy messersmith did something similar. He began his career as a performer playing in coffee shops. "Every gig you play leads to the next gig," he tells me. "You start small and make incremental changes." By the time he found himself performing live on the *Late Show* for millions of viewers, he says he wasn't even that nervous. He had done enough preparation. "It felt like I was an athlete, and I'd been working up to this for a long time," he says.

You may not be giving a TED talk or performing on live television. But there are probably plenty of other things you face every day that make you nervous or put you in a full-on state of panic, like Susan. You may want to step out of your comfort zone and make a few new friends. You might want to say hello to that cute girl in your class. You may want to share your ideas in a staff meeting because you know they'll improve things. Whatever it is, don't let fear be the reason not to do it. Like Susan and jeremy, you can start small and slowly work your way up to the thing that scares you.

The second big idea I want to leave you with is this: live fearlessly. Of course, this doesn't mean you won't *feel* fear. You'll probably still feel plenty of it. But you never have to *give in* to those feelings. You can still speak up or reach out. Remember that your feelings of fear are just that—feelings. You don't have to listen to them. That's what living fearlessly is about.

More Resources

If you've enjoyed this book, visit IntrovertDear.com/ SecretLives. I've put more resources for you there—and some ways you can connect with other introverts.

Be as You Are

One day in eighth grade, while shopping with my friends at the mall, I found a blue T-shirt with the words "Be As You Are" printed on it. The shirt was not quite the right size for me—it was just a little bit too small. As a result, it stretched awkwardly across my chest, and I had to constantly keep pulling it down so my belly wouldn't peek out. My friends tried to talk me out of it. "Why would you want a shirt like *that*?" they giggled. But I bought it anyway. I wore it all the time, even for my class picture that year. Imagine this: a nerdy girl with a bad perm, acne, and glasses, wearing a tiny shirt. There was only the hint of a smile on my lips. It's a strange-looking picture, but looking at it reminds me of how far I've come.

I didn't fully understand it, but even then, I felt like that T-shirt held a secret to life. Many people were telling me to "come out of my shell" and "stop being so quiet." Other middle schoolers laughed and joked and talked with ease. They didn't hide away in their bedrooms—writing poetry, reading mystery novels, and daydreaming—when there was social fun to be had. I guess that T-shirt was the message to myself that I needed to hear. It just took me all these years to decipher it.

I still believe that tiny T-shirt holds a secret to life. So my last big idea for you is this: be as you are. If you like staying in on a Friday night, then stay in. If you need quiet time, then take it. Don't perpetually wear an extroverted mask because you think that's what you're supposed to do. If you do, you might find yourself deeply unfulfilled and unhappy, divorced from what really makes you *you*. You might find yourself in the situation *I* found myself in during my younger years—you might believe there is something seriously wrong with you. Rather than fighting your introverted nature, start working with it.

This advice may seem contradictory to what I just suggested about living fearlessly. But it's not. Living fearlessly is about not letting fear hold you back from the things you want. "Be as you are" is about giving yourself permission for quiet. Permission to be you, introversion and all.

BIBLIOGRAPHY AND SUGGESTED READING

Chapter 1: This Is for All the Quiet Ones

Laney, Marti Olsen. *The Introvert Advantage: How Quiet People Can Thrive in an Extrovert World.* New York: Workman, 2002.

Cain, Susan. *Quiet: The Power of Introverts in a World That Can't Stop Talking.* New York: Random House, 2013.

Helgoe, Laurie. *Introvert Power: Why Your Inner Life Is Your Hidden Strength.* Illinois: Sourcebooks, 2013.

Dembling, Sophia. *The Introvert's Way: Living a Quiet Life in a Noisy World.* New York: Penguin Group, 2012.

Green, John. "Thoughts from Places: The Tour." YouTube video, 2:28. Posted January 17, 2012. https://youtu.be/qy6Fd aJ6Ayc?list=UUGaVdbSav8xWuFWTadK6loA.

Ponari, Marta, Luigi Trojano, Dario Grossi, and Massimiliano Conson. "'Avoiding or Approaching Eyes'? Introversion/Extraversion Affects the Gaze-Cueing Effect." *Cognitive Processing* 14 (2013): 293–9. doi:10.1007/s10339-013-0559-z.

Leikas, Sointu, and Ville-Juhani Ilmarinen. "Happy Now, Tired Later? Extraverted and Conscientious Behavior Are Related to

Immediate Mood Gains, but to Later Fatigue." *Journal of Personality* (2016). doi:10.1111/jopy.12264.

Depue, Richard A., and Yu Fu. "On the Nature of Extraversion: Variation in Conditioned Contextual Activation of Dopamine-Facilitated Affective, Cognitive, and Motor Processes." *Frontiers in Human Neuroscience* 7 (2013): 288. doi:10.3389/fnhum.2013.00288.

Jung, Carl. *Collected Works of C.G. Jung, Volume 6: Psychological Types.* Princeton: Princeton University Press, 1971.

Chapter 2: The Science of Introversion

Kaufman, Scott Barry. "The Science of Introversion." Last modified May 14, 2016. http://scottbarrykaufman.com/resources/the-science-of-introversion.

Schwartz, Ariel. "A Personality Psychologist Details the Differences between Introverts and Extroverts—Including How Often They Have Sex." *Business Insider*, February 19, 2016. http://www.businessinsider.com/difference-in-the-amount-of-sex-of-extroverts-and-introverts-2016-2.

Cohen, Michael X., Jennifer Young, Jong-Min Baek, Christopher Kessler, and Charan Ranganath. "Differences in Extraversion and Dopamine Genetics Predict Neural Reward Responses." *Cognitive Brain Research* 25, no. 3 (2005): 851–61. doi:10.1016/j.cogbrainres.2005.09.018.

DeYoung, Colin. Interview by author. Email. August 6, 2016.

Snidman, Nancy. Interview by author. Email. August 19, 2016.

Soto, Christopher. "Personality Can Change Over a Lifetime, and Usually for the Better." *NPR*, June 30, 2016. http://www.npr.org/sections/health-shots/2016/06/30/484053435/personality-can-change-over-a-lifetime-and-usually-for-the-better.

Roberts, Brent W., Dustin Wood, and Jennifer L. Smith. "Evaluating Five Factor Theory and Social Investment Perspectives on Personality Trait Development." *Journal of Research in Personality* 39, no. 1 (2005): 166–84. doi:10.1016/j.jrp.2004.08.002.

Hanson, Rick. *Hardwiring Happiness: The New Brain Science of Contentment, Calm, and Confidence.* New York: Penguin, 2013.

Hudson, Nathan W., and Chris R. Fraley. "Volitional Personality Trait Change: Can People Choose to Change Their Personality Traits?" *Journal of Personality and Social Psychology* 109, no. 3 (2015): 490–507. doi:10.1037/pspp0000021.

Specht, Jule, Boris Egloff, and Stefan C. Schmukle. "Examining Mechanisms of Personality Maturation." *Social Psychological and Personality Science* 4, no. 2 (2012): 181–9. doi:10.1177/1948550612448197.

Sólo, Andre. Interview by author. Personal interview. December 30, 2016.

Cheek, Jonathan M., Courtney A. Brown, and Jennifer O. Grimes. *Personality Scales for Four Domains of Introversion: Social, Thinking, Anxious, and Restrained Introversion.* Wellesley, MA: Department of Psychology, Wellesley College, 2014. https://www.academia.edu/7353616/

Laney, Marti Olsen. *The Introvert Advantage: How Quiet People Can Thrive in an Extrovert World.* New York: Workman Publishing, 2002.

Chapter 3: Introverts Are Rude (and Other Misconceptions)

Siegman, Aron W., and Theodore M. Dembroski. *In Search of Coronary-Prone Behavior: Beyond Type A.* Hillsdale: Lawrence Erlbaum Associates, 1989.

Chapman, Leanne. "Just Because I Don't Look Excited Doesn't Mean I'm Not Into This." *Introvert, Dear,* May 23, 2016. https://introvertdear.com/news/just-because-i-dont-look-excited-doesnt-mean-im-not-into-this/.

Chung, Michaela. *The Irresistible Introvert: Harness the Power of Quiet Charisma in a Loud World.* Skyhorse Publishing, 2016.

Bukowski, Charles. *Barfly.* DVD. Directed by Barbet Schroeder. Los Angeles: Paramount, 1987.

Cain, Susan. "Are You Shy, Introverted, Both, or Neither (And Why Does It Matter)?" *Psychology Today,* July 6, 2011. https://www.psychologytoday.com/blog/quiet-the-power-introverts/201107/are-you-shy-introverted-both-or-neither-and-why-does-it.

Jones, Del. "Not All Successful CEOS Are Extroverts." *USA Today,* June 7, 2006. http://usatoday30.usatoday.com/money/companies/management/2006-06-06-shy-ceo-usat_x.htm.

Q&A. "An Audience With Bill Gates." ABC, May 28, 2013. http://www.abc.net.au/tv/qanda/txt/s3761763.htm.

Weisberg, Jacob. "Yahoo's Marissa Mayer: Hail to the Chief." *Vogue*, August 15, 2013. http://www.vogue.com/article/hail-to-the-chief-yahoos-marissa-mayer.

Shear, Michael D. "Obama After Dark: The Precious Hours Alone." *New York Times*, July 2, 2016. https://www.nytimes.com/2016/07/03/us/politics/obama-after-dark-the-precious-hours-alone.html.

Miel, Virginia. "Don't Call Me Boring Because I Don't Like Parties." *Introvert, Dear*, July 29, 2016. https://introvertdear.com/news/dont-call-me-boring-because-i-dont-like-parties/.

Chapter 4: Yes, the "Introvert Hangover" Is Real

Courter, Shawna. "Yes, There Is Such a Thing as an 'Introvert' Hangover." *Introvert, Dear*, August 11, 2016. https://introvertdear.com/news/yes-there-is-such-a-thing-as-an-introvert-hangover/.

Stillman, Jessica. "Feeling Rough After an Event? You Might Have an 'Introvert Hangover'." *Inc.* magazine, August 25, 2016. https://www.inc.com/jessica-stillman/feeling-rough-after-an-event-you-might-have-an-introvert-hangover.html.

Singal, Jesse. "Introvert Hangovers Can Be Really Rough." *New York* magazine, August 15, 2016. http://nymag.com/scienceofus/2016/08/introvert-hangovers.html.

Knowles, Brenda. "Introvert Explained: Why We Love You But Need to Get Away From You." *Space2live Blog*, March 22, 2013. http://brendaknowles.com/introverts-explained-why-we-love-you-but-need-to-get-away-from-you/.

Chung, Michaela. "Introvert: How To Cure A Social Hangover." *Introvert Spring.* http://introvertspring.com/introvert-how-to-cure-a-social-hangover/.

Rauch, Jonathan. "Caring for Your Introvert." *The Atlantic,* March 2003. https://www.theatlantic.com/magazine/archive/2003/03/caring-for-your-introvert/302696/.

Ginder, Rachel. "Introverts, You Gotta Fight For Your Right Not to Party." *Introvert, Dear,* October 28, 2016. https://introvertdear.com/news/introverts-fight-for-your-right-not-to-party/.

Chapter 5: Introverts Aren't Unsociable—We Socialize Differently

Pinkney, Daniel. "8 Life and Work Issues as an INFJ." *MisterP.ink Blog,* March 18, 2016. http://www.misterp.ink/8-life-and-work-issues-as-an-infj/.

Fleeson, William, Adriane B. Malanos, and Noelle M. Achille. "An Intraindividual Process Approach to the Relationship between Extraversion and Positive Affect: Is Acting Extraverted as 'Good' as Being Extraverted?" *Journal of Personality and Social Psychology* 83, no. 6 (2003): 1409-22. doi:10.1037/0022-3514.83.6.1409.

Courter, Shawna. "I Wish I Hadn't Let Fear Stop Me From Making Friends." *Introvert, Dear,* August 30, 2016. https://introvertdear.com/news/i-wish-i-hadnt-let-fear-stop-me-from-making-friends/.

McHugh, Adam. Interview by author. Email. December 26, 2016.

Mehl, Matthias R., Simine Vazire, Shannon E. Holleran, and C. Shelby Clark. "Eavesdropping on Happiness: Well-Being Is Related to Having Less Small Talk and More Substantive Conversations." *Psychological Science* 21, no. 4 (2010): 539–41. doi:10.1177/0956797610362675.

Rabin, Roni Caryn. "Talk Deeply, Be Happy?" *New York Times*, March 17, 2010. https://well.blogs.nytimes.com/2010/03/17/talk-deeply-be-happy/?_r=0.

Chung, Michaela. *The Irresistible Introvert: Harness the Power of Quiet Charisma in a Loud World*. New York: Skyhorse Publishing, 2016.

Sevier, Maleri. "An Open Letter to INFJs Who Have Lost Close Friendships." *Introvert, Dear*, September 13, 2016. https://introvertdear.com/news/an-open-letter-to-infjs-who-have-lost-close-friendships/.

Chapter 6: Please Just Leave Me Alone

Ginder, Rachel. "I Wasn't Living My Life Until I Learned to Stay Home." *Introvert, Dear*, August 9, 2016. https://introvertdear.com/news/i-wasnt-living-my-life-until-i-learned-to-stay-home/.

Buchholz, Ester. "The Call of Solitude." *Psychology Today*, January 1, 1998. https://www.psychologytoday.com/articles/199801/the-call-solitude.

Neyfakh, Leon. "The power of lonely." *Boston Globe*, March 6, 2011. http://archive.boston.com/bostonglobe/ideas/articles/2011/03/06/the_power_of_lonely/?page=1.

Rumi, Jalal al-Din. *The Essential Rumi.* Translated by Coleman Barks, John Moyne, A. J. Arberry, and Reynold Nicholson. London: Penguin, 1995.

Arum, Richard, and Josipa Roksa. *Academically Adrift: Limited Learning on College Campuses.* Chicago: The University of Chicago Press, 2011.

Ratner, Rebecca K., and Rebecca W. Hamilton. "Why You're Better Off Going Alone Than Not at All." *Los Angeles Times,* May 29, 2015. http://www.latimes.com/opinion/op-ed/la-oe-ratnerhamilton-going-out-alone-20150531-story.html.

Sólo, Andre. Interview by author. Personal interview. December 30, 2016.

Fishman, Inna, Rowena Ng, and Ursula Bellugi. "Do Extraverts Process Social Stimuli Differently from Introverts?" *Cognitive Neuroscience* 2, no. 2 (2011): 67–73. doi:10.1080/1758 8928.2010.527434.

Hazlett, J. Lee. "An Open Letter to ISTJs on the Dangers of Obligations." *Introvert, Dear,* November 29, 2016. https://introvertdear.com/news/istj-dangers-of-obligation-open-letter/.

Jobs, Steve. "Q&A Session." Apple Worldwide Developers Conference, San Jose, May 6, 1997.

messersmith, jeremy. Interview by author. Personal interview. November 16, 2016.

Knowles, Brenda. "The Introvert's Love Affair with Solitude: Will It Always Be Taboo?" *Space2live Blog,* August 9, 2013. http://brendaknowles.com/the-introverts-love-affair-with-solitude-will-it-always-be-taboo-2/.

Kremer, William and Claudia Hammond. "Hikikomori: Why Are So Many Japanese Men Refusing to Leave Their Rooms?" *BBC World Service*, July 5, 2013. http://www.bbc.com/news/magazine-23182523.

Marano, Hara Estroff. "The Dangers of Loneliness." *Psychology Today*, June 9, 2016. https://www.psychologytoday.com/articles/200307/the-dangers-loneliness.

Archer, Dale. "Loneliness and Death." *Psychology Today*, April 23, 2015. https://www.psychologytoday.com/blog/reading-between-the-headlines/201504/loneliness-and-death.

Pappas, Stephanie. "7 Ways Friendships Are Great for Your Health." *Live Science*, January 8, 2016. http://www.livescience.com/53315-how-friendships-are-good-for-your-health.html.

Rowan, Karen. "Loneliness Linked with Dementia Risk." *Live Science*, December 11, 2012. http://www.livescience.com/25446-loneliness-feelings-dementia-risk.html.

Chapter 7: Let's Be Awkward Together—Dating for Introverts

Kelly, Anita E. "How to End Up With the Right Partner." *Psychology Today*, April 25, 2014. https://www.psychologytoday.com/blog/insight/201404/how-end-the-right-partner.

Zawila, Steven. Interview by author. Email. December 15, 2016.

Brafman, Rom. "The Virtues of Being Picky." *Psychology Today*, August 25, 2008. https://www.psychologytoday.com/blog/dont-be-swayed/200808/the-virtues-being-picky.

Zawila, Steven. "How to Be More Confident Around Women as an Introverted Man." *Introvert, Dear,* January 18, 2017. https://introvertdear.com/news/introverted-man-confident-around-women/.

Cain, Susan. *Quiet: The Power of Introverts in a World That Can't Stop Talking.* New York: Broadway Books, 2012.

Zawila, Steven. "The Introverted Man's Guide to Talking to Women." *Introvert, Dear,* May 18, 2016. https://introvertdear.com/news/introverted-mans-guide-to-talking-to-women/.

Chung, Michaela. *The Irresistible Introvert: Harness the Power of Quiet Charisma in a Loud World.* New York: Skyhorse Publishing, 2016.

Chapter 8: Let's Be Quiet Together—Introverts in Relationships

Lidnin, Alex. "Why I'll Forever Be Thankful for the Extrovert Who Interrupted My Reading." *Introvert, Dear,* November 23, 2016. https://introvertdear.com/news/why-ill-forever-be-thankful-for-the-extrovert-who-interrupted-my-reading/.

Porter, Aute. "How to Deal With Unrequited Love as an INFP." *Introvert, Dear,* December 9, 2016. https://introvertdear.com/news/infp-personality-type-unrequited-love/.

Sodermans, An Katrien, Martine Corijn, Sofie Vanassche, and Koen Matthijs. "Effects of Personality on Postdivorce Partnership Trajectories." *Journal of Social and Personal Relationships* (2016). doi:10.1177/0265407516665250.

Lewandowski, Gary and Nicole Bizzoco. "through Subtraction: Growth Following the Dissolution of a Low Quality

Relationship." *The Journal of Positive Psychology* 2, no. 1 (2007): 40–54. doi:10.1080/17439760601069234.

Erbentraut, Joseph. "How Long It REALLY Takes To Get Over A Breakup." *Huffington Post,* July 17, 2014. http://www.huffingtonpost.com/2014/07/17/corinne-mucha-get-over-it_n_5592469.html.

Fisher, Bruce, and Robert Alberti. "Recovering from Divorce." *Divorce Magazine,* March 20, 2017. http://www.divorcemag.com/articles/recovering-from-divorce.

Gračanin, Asmir, Ad J. J. M. Vingerhoets, Igor Kardum, Marina Zupčić, Maja Šantek, and Mia Šimić. "Why Crying Does and Sometimes Does Not Seem to Alleviate Mood: A Quasi-Experimental Study." *Motivation and Emotion* (2015). doi: 10.1007/s11031-015-9507-9.

Lieberman, Matthew D., Naomi I. Eisenberger, Molly J. Crockett, Sabrina M. Tom, Jennifer H. Pfeifer, and Baldwin M. Way. "Putting Feelings Into Words: Affect Labeling Disrupts Amygdala Activity in Response to Affective Stimuli." *Psychological Science* 18, no. 5 (2007): 421–8.

Klinenberg, Eric. *Going Solo: The Extraordinary Rise and Surprising Appeal of Living Alone.* New York: Penguin, 2012.

Brown, Amelia. "An Open Letter to Single INFJs." *Introvert, Dear,* March 9, 2016. https://introvertdear.com/news/open-letter-to-single-infjs/.

Chapter 9: Troubleshooting Your Relationship

Knowles, Brenda. "I'm Sorry I Hurt You in Order to Save Myself: What Introverts Feel but Don't Always Say." *Space2live*

Blog, August 23, 2015. http://brendaknowles.com/im-sorry-i-hurt-you-in-order-to-save-myself-what-introverts-feel-but-dont-always-say/.

Knowles, Brenda. "About." *Space2live Blog.* http://brendaknowles.com/about/.

Sólo, Andre. "5 Signs You're in the Right Relationship." *Introvert, Dear,* May 13, 2016. https://introvertdear.com/news/5-signs-youre-right-relationship/.

Whitbourne, Susan Krauss. "5 Relationship Red Flags You Need to Watch Out For." *Psychology Today,* October 17, 2005. https://www.psychologytoday.com/blog/fulfillment-any-age/201510/5-relationship-red-flags-you-need-watch-out.

Gottman, John. "What Makes Marriage Work?" *Psychology Today,* March 1, 1994. https://www.psychologytoday.com/articles/199403/what-makes-marriage-work.

Ni, Preston C. *Seven Keys to Long-Term Relationship Success.* Preston Ni Communication Coaching, 2012. E-reader edition.

Lisitsa, Ellie. "Manage Conflict: The Six Skills." *Gottman Relationship Blog.* https://www.gottman.com/blog/manage-conflict-the-six-skills/.

Chapter 10: Do I Really Have to Do This Again Tomorrow? Introverts and Career

Mueller, Kayla. "Just Because I Need Time to Respond Doesn't Mean I'm Unintelligent." *Introvert, Dear,* December 22, 2016.

https://introvertdear.com/news/introvert-time-to-respond-doesnt-mean-unintelligent/.

Lehrer, Jonah. "Brainstorming: An Idea Past Its Prime." *Washington Post,* April 19, 2012. https://www.washingtonpost.com/opinions/brainstorming-an-idea-past-its-prime/2012/04/19/gIQAhKT5TT_story.html?utm_term=.94fb30f48099.

Bendersky, Corinne and Neha Parikh Shah. "The Downfall of Extraverts and Rise of Neurotics: The Dynamic Process of Status Allocation in Task Groups." *The Academy of Management Journal* 56, no 2. (2012): 387–406. doi:10.5465/amj.2011.0316.

Bruzzese, Anita. "On the Job: Introverts Win in the End." *USA Today,* April 28, 2013. https://www.usatoday.com/story/money/columnist/bruzzese/2013/04/28/on-the-job-introverts-vs-extroverts/2114539/.

Sweeney, Colleen. "As an Introvert, Working in Retail Was a Nightmare." *Introvert, Dear,* September 22, 2016. https://introvertdear.com/news/working-in-retail-was-a-nightmare-for-me-as-an-introvert/.

Ancowitz, Nancy. Interview by author. Email. December 28, 2016.

Lee, Tony. "The Best Jobs for Introverts." *CareerCast Blog.* http://www.careercast.com/jobs-rated/best-jobs-introverts.

Chapter 11: Troubleshooting Your Job

Hazlett, J. Lee. "Inside the Mind of an Introverted Property Manager on Rent Day." *Introvert, Dear,* August 25, 2016. https://

introvertdear.com/news/inside-the-mind-of-an-introvert-property-manager-on-rent-day/.

Stanton, Hayley. "5 Things Introverts Wish Job Interviewers Knew." *Introvert, Dear*, August 3, 2016. https://introvertdear.com/news/5-things-introverts-wish-job-interviewers-knew/.

Smith, Tobie. "Why Job Interviews Can Be Hard for Introverts (and What to Do About It)." *Introvert, Dear*, May 29, 2015. https://introvertdear.com/news/why-introverts-struggle-with-promoting-themselves-in-job-interviews/.

McBeth, Katie. "4 Talking Points That Will Help You Sell Your Introvert Skills in a Job Interview." *Introvert, Dear*, October 5, 2016. https://introvertdear.com/news/4-talking-points-that-will-help-you-sell-your-introvert-skills-in-a-job-interview/.

Razavi, Katrina. "How to Network Without Changing Who You Are." *Introvert, Dear*, September 6, 2016. https://introvertdear.com/news/how-to-network-while-staying-true-to-your-introverted-nature/.

Chapter 12: Inside the Introvert's Inner World

messersmith, jeremy. Interview by author. Personal interview. November 16, 2016.

Cain, Susan. "The Rise of the New Groupthink." *New York Times*, January 13, 2012. http://www.nytimes.com/2012/01/15/opinion/sunday/the-rise-of-the-new-groupthink.html.

Neyfakh, Leon. "The Power of Lonely." *Boston Globe*, March 6, 2011. http://archive.boston.com/bostonglobe/ideas/articles/2011/03/06/the_power_of_lonely/?page=1.

Rhimes, Shonda. *Year of Yes: How to Dance It Out, Stand in the Sun and Be Your Own Person.* New York: Simon and Schuster, 2015.

Hammel, Sara, and Lesley Messer. "Courteney Cox and David Arquette Get On-Air Marriage Counseling." *People*, September 23, 2016. http://people.com/celebrity/courteney-cox-and-david-arquette-get-on-air-marriage-counseling/.

Day, Felicia. *You're Never Weird on the Internet (Almost): A Memoir.* New York: Touchstone, 2015.

Cain, Susan. *Quiet: The Power of Introverts in a World that Can't Stop Talking.* New York: Broadway Books, 2012.

Rampton, John. "23 of the Most Amazingly Successful Introverts in History." *Inc.* https://www.inc.com/john-rampton/23-amazingly-successful-introverts-throughout-history.html.

Dreher, Beth. "9 People You'd Never Guess Were Introverts." *Reader's Digest.* http://www.rd.com/culture/famous-introverts/.

Rowling, J.K. *J.K. Rowling's Blog.* https://www.jkrowling.com.

Hemingway, Ernest. "Nobel Prize Acceptance Speech." Nobel Prize Banquet, Stockholm, December 10, 1954.

Wozniak, Steve. *iWoz: Computer Geek to Cult Icon.* New York: W. W. Norton & Company, 2006.

Cummings, E. E. "The Agony of the Artist (with a Capital A)." *Vanity Fair*, April 1927.

Zazzara, Lauren. "I'm an INFJ, and I Have Resting Sad Face." *Introvert, Dear*, August 2, 2016. https://introvertdear.com/news/im-an-infj-and-i-have-resting-sad-face/.

Morin, Amy. *13 Things Mentally Strong People Don't Do: Take Back Your Power, Embrace Change, Face Your Fears, and Train Your Brain for Happiness and Success.* New York: HarperCollins, 2014.

Michl, Louisa C., Katie A. McLaughlin, Kathrine Shepherd, and Susan Nolen-Hoeksema. "Rumination as a Mechanism Linking Stressful Life Events to Symptoms of Depression and Anxiety: Longitudinal Evidence in Early Adolescents and Adults." *Journal of Abnormal Psychology* 122, no. 2 (2013): 339–52. doi:10.1037/a0031994.

Thomsen, Dorthe Kirkegaard, Mimi Yung Mehlsen, Søren Christensen, and Robert Zachariae. "Rumination—Relationship with Negative Mood and Sleep Quality." *Personality and Individual Differences* 34, no. 7 (2003): 1293–1301. doi:10.1016/S0191-8869(02)00120-4.

Chapter 13: Work with Your Introversion Rather than Fight against It

Rendall, David J. *The Freak Factor: Discovering Uniqueness by Flaunting Weakness.* Charleston: Advantage, 2015.

Sapala, Lauren. "You're Not Responsible for Other People's Feelings." *Introvert, Dear,* August 19, 2016. https://introvertdear.com/news/youre-not-responsible-for-other-peoples-feelings/.

Cain, Susan. Interview by author. Email. January 25, 2017.

Cain, Susan. "The Power of Introverts." Filmed February 2012. TED video, 19:04. https://www.ted.com/talks/susan_cain_the_power_of_introverts.

ACKNOWLEDGMENTS

A big, heartfelt thanks to every introvert who shared their inner world with me. Our discussions were invaluable, and this book would not be a reality without you.

Thank you to Colin DeYoung, who patiently answered my questions, email after email. Thank you to Susan Cain, Nancy Snidman, Adam McHugh, Nancy Ancowitz, Steven Zawila, David Rendall, and Jonathan Cheek, who were wonderful resources while writing this book. Thank you to my editor, Kim Lim, who patiently endured my many panic-driven, last-minute edits. And to jeremy messersmith, who chatted with me over coffee at a Minnesota Bachman's, making my fangirl dream of meeting him come true.

Thank you to my parents, Steve and Marge Granneman, who raised me to love reading books and writing stories, and who made me believe that I could be anything I wanted to be, even a writer.

Thank you to Marti Olsen Laney, whose book first opened my eyes to introversion. Also, to Laurie Helgoe, Sophia Dembling, Susan Cain, Brenda Knowles, Michaela Chung, and so many others who are spreading the message of introvert self-love and acceptance.

Thank you to everyone in the *Introvert, Dear* community, as well as the many writers of *Introvert, Dear*, who bravely make some of their most personal thoughts and moments public by sharing them with the Internet.

Thanks to the technicians at the iShop in Querétaro, Mexico, who managed to recover the draft of my first few chapters from my laptop after I spilled a drink on it—all while putting up with my poor Spanish.

Thank you to my friends, who didn't hear from me much during the months I was glued to my laptop, writing and researching. Thank you to my boyfriend, Andre Sólo, who believed in me as an author even before I did. And to Mattie and Colmes, my cats, who often sat near my desk in solidarity as I wrote, and who didn't meow too much.